D0772036

LOST
IN SIN

JASON RANGEL

DISCARDED FROM
GARFIELD COUNTY PUBLIC
LIBRARY SYSTEM

Garfield County Libraries
Silt Branch Library
680 Home Avenue
Silt, CO 81652
(970) 876-5500 Fax (970) 876-5921
www.GCPLD.org

ISBN 978-1-63844-728-3 (paperback)
ISBN 978-1-63844-730-6 (hardcover)
ISBN 978-1-63844-729-0 (digital)

Copyright © 2021 by New Hope Film and Entertainment

All rights reserved. No part of this publication may be reproduced, distributed, or transmitted in any form or by any means, including photocopying, recording, or other electronic or mechanical methods without the prior written permission of the publisher. For permission requests, solicit the publisher via the address below.

Christian Faith Publishing, Inc.
832 Park Avenue
Meadville, PA 16335
www.christianfaithpublishing.com

Cover photos by Geovanny Flores
All other photos by Sarah Harms
Cover design by Mikel Saint

Printed in the United States of America

For Jocelyn, Noah, Jonah, and Helena.

CONTENTS

FOREWORD

It can't hurt to open it. You have now taken this book into your hands, and I do not believe it is by chance. I believe that God has placed this book into your life, as well as mine, to remind us of his great love. Yes, even when we are unlovable and we find ourselves in the lowest of lows, God's love is still available. As I found myself reading through *Lost in Sin*, I can testify that everything Jason wrote here is true. Having been his pastor for many years and knowing the family for over twenty-five years, Jason wrote his true-life story. I remember many moments when myself, as well as his parents, had continually prayed for Jason's salvation. I will say this, "Never give up on praying for your lost loved ones. God hears, and he will answer." I encourage you mother, father, and grandparent to keep the faith and pray without ceasing. Reading the story contained inside this book, you will be reminded as I was about the relentless love of God. That love that never gives up, that love that is willing to recover us from wherever we may find ourselves. This love, God's love, does not need for us to come cleansed and perfect, but as we are. Roman's 5:8 says, "But God demonstrates his own love for us in this: while we were still sinners, Christ died for us." I dare ask you, Why are you reading this book? Maybe because you need the words of this story to remind you that no matter how far you feel you are from God, his love for you is still calling you back. And if you have ever felt as if there is no hope, take it firsthand from Jason, there is still another chance. God will always have his arms wide open. Are you tired of the constant harassment of the enemy telling you that it is too late? Let this book be a reminder of a soul the devil thought he had won but in the end he had certainly lost. Jason is a living testimony of what God can do when we are willing to let go and trust him. Jason's story is not only of his sinful past but also of what God continues to do in his life. Jason has allowed God to use him not only in this book but also through music, the worship song "You Are You Are" he recorded while in preparation for the ministry. I have had the privilege of witnessing Jason's constant change as he walks this journey with God. So if God can reach out and change Jason, he can certainly do the same with you. I will challenge you to read this book in its entirety and share the story with someone else. Pass it on. There are many others around us that need a true story of hope, that salvation we can only find in Jesus. There is still an opportunity for you to come home... because he is calling you.

—Pastor Rigo Magana

"The Spirit of the Lord is upon me because the Lord has anointed me to preach good news to the poor; he has sent me to heal the brokenhearted, to proclaim freedom to the captives, and the opening of the prison to those who are bound; to proclaim the acceptable year of the Lord, and the day of vengeance of our God; to comfort all who mourn, to console those who mourn in Zion, to give them a crown of beauty instead of ashes, the oil of joy for mourning, the garment of praise instead of a spirit of heaviness; that they may be called trees of righteousness, the planting of the Lord, that he may be glorified."

—Isaiah 61:1–3

CHAPTER 1

The Beginning

My earliest memory as a child was accepting Jesus Christ as my Lord and Savior at the tender age of five. My wonderful Aunt Marlene who I loved very much was so enthused and excited to tell me an awesome story about a man who had lived and died two thousand years ago. It was a spring night, and I can still remember sitting in her blue Toyota Celica in a parking lot, talking. She explained to me that this man, who I never knew or met, had loved me so much that he had died for my sins and was resurrected three days later. My sins? Umm...now I guess I didn't really understand what a sin was at just five years old, but I understood this man had made a great sacrifice. She asked me if I wanted to accept this man in my heart. His name was Jesus Christ. I paused for a few seconds, thought about it, and then with all my innocence, I said yes. This was the beginning of my walk with Christ and would change the rest of my life indefinitely.

My father and mother divorced when I was just a baby, but I was definitely loved and cared for. I lived with my mother and my grandparents in a very small town about twenty miles north of Denver. My dad was an alcoholic and a womanizer at that time who rode a Harley and ran wild. They were married for about two and a half years when they eventually divorced and went their separate ways. My mother took me and moved back in with her parents and gave me a homelife the best she could. My grandpa Tony was a really good man who had seven children and many grandchildren with my grandmother Margaret. Living with my grandparents was a really good experience, and I would not trade those memories for the world. My grandpa ran a farm, and I would go with him sometimes and get to play with the dogs and ride on his tractor. My grandmother was a strong woman but very loving and caring; I was very close with her and even still to this day. I lived with my grandparents and my mother for the first five years of my life. I have very fond memories of my grandparent's house and the farm. Those two taught me a lot about hard work and family, life lessons that will never be forgotten.

I really don't remember my father when I was younger; the memories are very vague and few and far between, but I knew he always loved and cared for his one and only son. I do remember his mother and father, my grandparents, who were very loving and cared a lot about me. My grandpa Joe was a stubborn man who drank beer and cussed and was backsliding from church. My grandmother Helen was a deacon's daughter who served the Lord, and she's the very reason my family serves the Lord today. She was a prayer warrior and a Sunday school teacher who had a deep faith and served God with all her heart. She instilled a lot of my beliefs that I still carry with me even to this day. My grandfather Joe was a torn man who never really had peace or surrendered to God. He was womanizer and abusive to his family in his younger days. They had four children, including my father, and my grandmother was a faithful loving wife till the day she passed. But my memories of them were always good, and they loved me and treated me really well. I always had a good time when I was at my grandparents' home; I would see my dad there and spend time with him also. My childhood was filled with positive loving memories for the most part, but still I was a child of a broken family.

That all changed by the age of eight when my parents decided to reconcile and remarry, which was an awesome event. My father was a hardworking sober man by then who never really stayed with a company for too long but was never short of work. He worked in the oilfield and gave up drinking and his wild ways to work things out with my mom. He was instilled with very good values from his mother, and like his father, he was prone to addiction. But he was back for the long haul, and he took care of me and was by my mother's side and tried to finally be a family man. My mother had a very stable job, working for an insurance company. She was also a hard worker and a very dependable employee. Around that same time, my mother had given her life to the Lord, and we started attending a local church that my dad's family attended. We had moved to a larger college town about fifty miles north of Denver, but it was still pretty small comparatively. They rented till they eventually bought their first home in an upper-middle-class community, which changed my childhood drastically.

I started school there on the westside of town, and of course, I was the only Hispanic kid in an all-White class. So needless to say, it was a culture shock coming from the neighborhood before where everyone looked like me and was of the same ethnicity. I had a hard time fitting in and a really hard time making friends. This was the start of the fourth grade, and I was not ready for this type of racial rejection. I was very shy and insecure, and I looked different from everyone else in my new school. The kids were very entitled, cruel, and made fun of the way I looked. By the start of the fifth grade, it was only becoming worse, but I was still a straight-A student and loved to learn. My parents both worked very hard and tried to give me the very best they could. I was still serving the Lord wholeheartedly, and I talked to God every day and prayed for my loved ones and for my friends at school (even though I didn't really have any). I guess you could say I was a pretty good kid at the time and was just trying to find exactly where I fit in. I wasn't ready for what was coming in the next few years of my life, and it wasn't going to get any easier for me. I was a God-fearing, Jesus-loving, churching-going kid, and I was very smart but withheld. I had a calling in my life, and I wouldn't understand this till I was much older one day.

The fall of the sixth grade was the dawn of a prepubescent nightmare to say the very least. I was small for my age, and the other kids started hitting puberty and going through growth spurts. I was shy and insecure, and I really didn't know how to make any real friends or talk to anybody. I was still a straight-A student, but I was being bullied and picked on right from the get-go. I believe this is a real critical time for a kid and really starts to define you as a young adult and can affect you for years to come. My father had turned back to using drugs, and my mother was pregnant with my baby sister. I witnessed my dad being high and not in his right mind, and it scared me to death. This experience would affect me negatively for a long time. My dad would eventually end up in jail, and my pregnant mother and I were left all alone. At this same time, I was being picked on, and my self-esteem was very low. I was ashamed of the way I looked, and I was made fun of on a daily basis, and I did not feel very good about myself. I had strong Hispanic features, which included a wide nose, and my ears were something I was ashamed of. I remember being made fun of because of my ears sticking out, so I would tape them back at night, hoping somehow they would stay. But of course, they didn't, and so I would start daydreaming more and more and lose focus on what was really important like my schoolwork. I didn't know how to defend myself or speak up when someone ridiculed or bullied me out of fear of more rejection. I was scared to go to lunch and recess because I knew I would be sitting alone with only my thoughts, and I was embarrassed of having no one to talk to. This went on through the sixth and seventh grade and was it very hard for me to deal with. I was going to church with my mother and baby sister, and I was praying for my dad and my family. I was really sensitive to the Holy Spirit, and I would be overcome by it and fall slain in it. I was sent to youth conventions a couple times, where I was told I had a calling in my life. On one occasion, I had an evangelist pray for me and tell me I was gonna be a great evangelist one day for the Lord. And another time, an evangelist had told me that God told him I was going to be a pastor one day. But as a young teen, I just kind of blew it off and assumed they told everyone at youth conventions that, and it didn't really mean anything special. And I was so young, and I didn't really understand what they meant as they were prophesying over me. But soon after, my father was released from jail, and he went through addiction counseling and reconciled once again with my mother. He had recommitted his life back to Christ while he was behind bars, and he never looked back. My baby sister was now two years of age, and my family was complete again. By now, seventh grade was coming to an end, and eighth grade was going to be a whole new year and a whole new school… here we go junior high.

Now entering the eighth grade was an experience I was not ready for, and I was not expecting more bullying, but it was coming. As a fourteen-year-old young adult male, you are coming into your own existence in life, and it can be very cruel. Dressing the right way and wearing the right clothes becomes a very important factor in your day-to-day routine. Luckily I had parents who dressed me in decent clothing that I, of course, asked for, and they did their best to make that happen. I went from being made fun of everyday in middle school to being made fun of every other day in junior high. But I was physically changing, and puberty was treating me all right. I ended up in a couple of fistfights, but the outcome was not as bad as you would expect. By the end of the eighth grade, the cool kids started to accept me and talk to me, and I started making friends. About this same time, I started to notice the pretty females all around me, and of course, my grades started to take a dive. In junior high, the girls and boys started dating each other and walking down the halls, holding hands and passing notes. I was really enjoying my new found call of being a ladies' man, and I really wanted a girlfriend. Talking to females and befriending them came natural to me, and I was enjoying the pursuit. It wouldn't be until the following year where I would finally meet my very first real friend who happened to be a girl…hence, my first girlfriend.

It was the ninth grade, and I was really coming into my own and making multiple friends and allies. I started to defend myself in fights, and it was a good thing because I was getting into plenty of them weekly. The more someone bullied me or anyone else, the more I stuck up for them or myself. I had a very good sense of right and wrong, and I knew picking on someone and making fun of them for no reason was wrong. My grades were falling, but my self-confidence and self-esteem was rising, and I was not gonna go back. I was too naive to understand that you can have good grades, high self-esteem, and self-confidence all at the same time. I admire young people today that possess all those awesome qualities, sky's the limit for sure. But as for me, my mind was on the young females in my class. I would daydream about them and having them as my girlfriend. They were very pretty, and I was awestruck when one would give me a glance or even talk to me.

One fall day, in the beginning of the ninth grade season, I saw this cute little Hispanic girl, and she was very sweet and innocent. Our eyes met, and she smiled at me, and I smiled back at her, and I just knew she was gonna be my girl someday. It didn't take long before we became friends and started holding hands in the hallways and hanging out after school. I was fifteen years old and very eager to be accepted by whomever and whoever, and she was eager to accept me. She lived with her grandmother and baby sister, and her mother was in and out of her life. She was from a broken family too, and her father was never there for her or had anything to do with her. Her mother liked to go out and booze, and I just remember that little girl being very alone. But I really liked her, and we just kind of found each other and became close. What would happen next would change my mindset and life very drastically.

CHAPTER 2

A Falling

I can remember my relationship with this young lady starting off very innocent and nonchalant. She was one year younger than me, which made her fourteen. I was one year older and her very first boyfriend. I can still recall walking with her down the hallways and her giving me sweet little notes, saying that she loved me. One fall day, her friends and a couple of my friends dared us to kiss, and both of us had never kissed anyone before, so we were very nervous. She leaned forward and gave me a big soft smooch, and I was elated. Our young relationship was very peaceful and seemed so innocent to the people around us. My parents knew nothing about it, and her grandmother and mother were unaware of our friendship too. I was fifteen and in the ninth grade, and things were changing for me in good ways. I was still getting into a lot of fights, but I was not scared or afraid to fight back. And I have to explain something very crucial to my story. I was never a fighter or a tough kid at all. I hated confrontation for the most part, and I felt like fighting was pointless unless I had a real reason to be angry, and I didn't. Life was good, and my childhood was leaving my mind frame fast, and I started to become a young adult. My walk with God was getting weaker and weaker, and I was starting not to pray as often as I used too. My grades were dropping steadily, and I pretty much just lost all focus on the things that were meant to make me a successful person. I was fifteen and had gone through puberty a few years earlier when my dad was in jail, and my mom was preoccupied with having my baby sister. So I was a little bit angry, and maybe I was a little bit hurt. I guess deep down inside I was confused, and I just didn't know how to deal with it. So I really became quite infatuated with this young lady very fast, and it didn't take long before we started having sex.

It was the first time for both of us, and we were both really scared and nervous. I can remember praying to God and telling him what I was about to do, and that I was leaving him for a while. I was tired of being a good kid, and I wanted to have sex with this young lady and that was that. I told him I would come back when I was 30, and there it was, I no longer wanted to be a Christian. But sitting here looking back at my life, I can't help but to think that was a very sad day. I gave it all up for a relationship with a young female, and that was the biggest mistake I would ever make in my life. But it had to occur, and I wouldn't be who I am today if it wouldn't have happened the way it did. But to anybody reading this book, I pray you never sacrifice your personal relationship with Jesus Christ for no man or woman. It's the most important relationship you will ever have in your life, and it is very sacred. But I did it. I gave up my walk with Christ for this young woman, and life went on. We would walk after school to her house, and she would sneak me in, and we would kiss and have sex. Or I would meet her at the movies, and we would ditch our friends and walk to a nearby park and be together in the grass under a tree. I never looked back. I was hurt with my father, and I was angry, and I guess this was my escape or my way of lashing out. But I was opening doors that I couldn't close, and with sexual sin comes a very heavy price tag. My dad never talked to me about sex or told me anything about using protection, and I believe he was totally unaware of what was happening in my life. He worked a lot, and he was always tired when he wasn't working, so dealing with me was something he kind of left to my mom. And she was unaware of anything I was doing because she worked a lot also, so they would ask me how I was doing in school, and I would always say I was doing fine. And they took what I said at face value, not realizing my school work was not being completed, and I was ditching my classes. The summer after ninth grade was a long one, and I was always with this girl, and we were together constantly. My parents had finally met her and thought she was cute and were okay with us being friends and hanging out. I had met her mother and grandmother, and they were not too happy, but in the end, everyone was okay with us dating.

I was going into high school, and she was gonna start the ninth grade when the worst finally happened. I can't really recall how it all went down, but I can remember her inviting me to her house and telling me she was pregnant. I was oblivious to the fact that this could even happen as a result of us having a sexual relationship. She was so scared, and her mom already knew about the pregnancy, and she was not very happy. In fact, she was furious. She told me her dad also knew, and even though he was not in the picture, her mother had already called and told him. I was supposed to go home and tell my parents, but of course, I did nothing of the sort. A few days later, they all showed up at my parents' home, and she was very scared and sad. Her father and mother came in with her, and my parents were not expecting any of the news they were about to hear. Her dad didn't say too much, and I can remember her mom doing all the talking. They told my unassuming parents that their daughter, who had just turned fifteen, had become pregnant by me. My parents were very shocked to hear this news and were even more devastated when they heard she was not gonna keep it. Her mother said she was making her daughter have an abortion, and that was that. I can remember my mother and father pleading with her parents, saying they would raise the baby and to please not abort it. My parents were good people, my dad was serving the Lord now, and they both were going to church. I had stopped going to church with them, but they hadn't given up on me. Her parents said no and also said their daughter, and I were done as they stood up and walked out the door with her. I was just sixteen years old when this all happened, naive to say the very least and very immature. I had just started high school.

I can still remember the gloomy day when this young lady had called me and told me she had the abortion. She was crying and very upset, and she had told me she was tired and didn't feel very good. I was very sad for her, but the fact that we both had created a little life, and that it no longer existed on this earth didn't seem real to me. She and I tried to stay together afterward, but that experience changed her for the worse, and she really took a left. She eventually got into heavy drugs and drinking and hanging out with a bad crowd. I broke up with her later that year while I was still a sophomore, and I can still remember the look on her face. It was a sad ending to something that started so innocent and happy and would pretty much set up the rest of my young life and hers. She went on a downward spiral and went off the deep end, and she started to sink into depression. I really don't know what happened to her after that whole ordeal, but I assumed the worst. I never talked to her again because we had a bad falling out, and she went as far as accusing me of some bad things that I didn't do. She was using drugs, and I didn't like that and kicked her out my parents' house when she came over high and wanting to trade sex for money. I feel bad for that young woman and pray that she is doing okay and has found peace in her life. I was careless and I did some really dumb things as a kid, and it was hard to forgive myself and to forgive her.

I went back to trying to function through high school, trying to fit in, ditching class, and dating other females. I also started to hang out with a bad crowd, and I was willing to do whatever it took to be cool. I started to grow my hair long and sag my pants and basically just try to find my identity. These kids that I admired and wanted to be like were stoners and had long hair and listened to rock music and were into the grunge scene. I was still getting into a lot of fistfights with the Hispanic cholos because I hung out with these people.

One day, I decided to ditch class with these guys, and one of these kids pulled out a joint and started to pass it around. I felt so nervous and insecure, and I was not sure what I was gonna do next. But eventually it was passed to me, and of course, I wanted to fit in so bad that I took a hit and passed it on. I had never done drugs at this point of my life, but it was something that was destined to cross my path. My parents once again had never talked to me about peer pressure or doing drugs, and I'm pretty sure that was the last thing on their minds at the time. I was still a good kid for the most part, but I was headed down a wrong path that had no exits as far as anyone was concerned. I was rebelling against school, my parents, basically against God and his call on my life. I wanted nothing more to do with him, and all I wanted was to be accepted and to fit in. But I didn't fit in. I was not cool; I was basically a wannabe and now a drug user who was failing high school. And still I was always thinking about the females in my class, not the average ones but ones that were really beautiful and out of my league.

I had met a really pretty girl toward the middle of my sophomore year who really liked me, and we started hanging out and kissing in the halls. The only thing that she forgot to tell me was that she was engaged to some older guy, and he was a senior and a black belt in karate. One day, she found me, and we started talking, and she leaned over grabbed me, and we started kissing in the lunchroom. The next thing I knew I was being picked up and thrown through the school trophy case. Glass went flying everywhere, and all the kids in the lunchroom started yelling and laughing hysterically. This guy was screaming and crying and asking her why. She told him it was my fault, so he continued to pummel me. He was six foot two and a little out of my weight class, and let's just say I was lucky to get up and go to my next period. But minutes later, I was pulled out and sent to the principal's office. This young man who had beaten me up was not in trouble, but of course, I was. He was the principal's best friend's son, and I was told I was getting expelled from high school. I can remember my father having to come pick me up and the principal telling him that was my third fight that year, and I was done. He forced my dad to withdraw me from that high school and find a different one. As I was leaving, that kid and his girlfriend were laughing at me and flipped me off. It was a sad, pathetic day for me and a real low point that I will never understand or forget. I was making a lot of bad choices, and my grades were all failing. My parents assumed I could pull myself out of this, but I was headed on a downward spiral that I couldn't pull myself out of. I needed to repent to God at this point and get back to the basics of serving him wholeheartedly. But that was no longer an option for me because I had my mind made up that I was gonna be cool, and I wanted to finally fit in. I was soon finding myself getting ready to start a new school and having to start all over again.

My dad had bought me a car for my seventeenth birthday, and I was working a part-time job and getting ready to start the eleventh grade. I was ready to do good at this new school and was excited to start some place where nobody knew who I was or where I had been. I could be anybody at this new school, and I wanted to be somebody, and I wanted to be cool. It started off great, and I was excited by the new opportunity to change my life and get good grades. The first week there, I met and made some new friends immediately, and everyone treated me well. I was going to all my classes and doing my homework every single night. I had cut my hair and had a new style, and I was feeling really good about myself.

The start of the second week, I was going to my locker when this girl at the locker next to me accidentally dropped her books, and I instinctively dropped down to help her pick them up. When I came up, my jaw dropped, and standing in front of me was the prettiest little blond female I had ever seen in my life thus far. She looked like a movie star, and she was very humble and shy.

She said "thank you" as I was giving her books back to her.

I smiled at her and said, "You're welcome," and she hurried off to class. I couldn't stop thinking about her, and she was everything a guy would want as a girlfriend in high school. She was really petite and dressed really cute. I believe the movie *Clueless* was out at the time, and she took a fashion note from that film. Weeks went by, and I would catch this young woman staring at me as I walked down the halls, and she was always smiling. If I were smarter, I would have realized this young lady liked me, and I should have gone and talked to her. This girl was hands down the prettiest girl at West High, and I can remember all the girls talking about her and the football players trying to date her. I was doing good and feeling good, and of course, people and women are attracted to confidence and someone who's winning. It was a couple weeks into the school year, and I was walking down the hallway, talking to some friends when this young lady walked up to me and told me hi. I smiled back at her and nodded my head as she nervously smiled back. She right away began telling me that she thought I was cute and if I had anybody to take to home-coming. I was so flattered and excited that this particular person was asking me that I blurted out, "No, just you!"

She said, "Okay," smiled, and walked away.

Everybody in that vicinity had witnessed this occurrence, and by the next week, this girl and I were holding hands and passing notes in the hallways. I became popular all because I was dating this young woman, and it felt great because I was finally getting what I had always wanted…acceptance. I can remember my dad dropping something off for me at school one day, and I was talking to him, and he saw her and said, "Wow, who is that?"

I smiled and told him that she was my homecoming date and my new girlfriend. It felt good, and I was proud to have her on my arm and to get the approval of someone like my father.

But everything was gonna come crashing down around me, a pattern that my life would follow for many years to come. Nothing good can last forever, right? That's something that was instilled in me from a very young age. See, being cool and popular and dating the prettiest girl at West High meant that people were gonna start invit-ing you to parties and offering you drugs and alcohol. And I had a real problem saying no to anything anyone offered me because of my low self-esteem and wanting to fit in so bad. The jocks started offer-ing me weed, the stoners started offering me weed, and the cholos, well, they started offering me weed. And before I knew it, I was high at high school, before school, and after school, and my grades started to take a dive again. I started ditching class and going out to the parking lot and getting high and only coming back to walk my new girlfriend to her next class. Then I would be off ditching class again to go get high some more with someone else. I thought about it for many years after…why couldn't I have just been happy and satisfied with what I had? Why couldn't I have just said no and gone to class and been successful in school? Why? Why? Why? So many regrets but the worst was yet to come that school year.

Homecoming was coming up, and this girl was so excited for us to go together, and I am not gonna lie…so was I. On the day of homecoming, I went to the mall with my cousin who was to say the least, a semiprofessional thief and a good one. He came from a family that wasn't doing as well as my family was at the time, and kind of learned to take what he needed or what he didn't need he still took. My parents were excited for me to take my pretty date to homecoming and gave me money to buy some new clothes. But my cousin who came with me was stealing everything that wasn't nailed down, bad choice to bring him that day for sure. I saw this really expensive jacket on the rack, and I was gonna buy it. But my cousin somehow, probably rather easily, convinced me to steal it. I put the jacket on and walked right out the door like the dumb kid I had proven myself to be. As soon as I had gotten through the outside doors, security grabbed me and walked me straight to the back. By the time they scolded me and called my parents to come down and get me, it was already time to pick up my date. My parents probably believed whatever story I told them and gave me the keys to their car to go to homecoming. I was an hour and a half late, and suffice to say, she wasn't very happy at all. We opted not to go to the school dance, and instead we went to the park to drink and make out. Little did I realize that was gonna be the last time I was gonna get to hang out with her.

By Monday morning, she had broken up with me, and she was dating one of the jocks by Monday afternoon. Whatever I was projecting, she didn't like, and she was smart enough to spot a sinking ship in an ocean of lies. I was putting up a facade, and I did not possess the skills needed to be what I was trying to be. I had major regret; it was a cruel blow to my somehow oversized inflated ego.

At this point, I was failing all my classes again, and I was at the point of no return. I watched this woman be swept away by someone else, and I guess hurt and anger started to fill my heart. But not at myself like it should have been, but I felt like this hurt and anger was toward the women in my life. And it was not full-blown at this point, but this was the start of something worse to come. But it was all my doing, of course, and I needed direction, I needed guidance, and especially I needed God. My mom and dad were busy working away, trying to give me and my baby sister the best life they could. But I was steadily slippin' through the cracks, and without someone to really see what was going on, I wasn't going to make it.

I can remember getting so high in the parking lot at school and walking into the building, not knowing what class I was supposed to be in. A true nightmare that would haunt me for years to come. I would have these dreams constantly where I was lost and couldn't find my way to class. I would wake up sweating and in turmoil, but instead of praying to God like I should have, I would just turn around and go back to bed. I had gotten so far behind in my schoolwork that my teachers saw no hope for me passing any of my classes.

About that same time, my after-school job fired me for coming to work high, so high they immediately asked me to leave. The next day, I went to school, and they called me into the principal's office, and boy was I sweating bricks. My heart felt so heavy I could feel God calling me to come back, but I was so far gone at this point and stubborn that there was no going back. I came into his office and sat down, sweating profusely and nervous. It started like all these conversations start.

"How are you doing? We need to talk with you."

You could feel the heaviness in the room, and you could cut the tension with a knife.

The principle looked right at me and said, "There is no hope for you, my man, you're too far behind. Summer school is no option, and we are asking you to leave this school."

It was cold and straight to the point with no hope because certainly at this time, I was hopeless. I walked out of that office with my head down, realizing I had started off that year so positive and full of promise. But this pattern in my life was going to follow me for a very long time to come and with much greater adversity. This was such a critical moment in my life. This was the time when I should have been thinking about going to school dances, playing sports, and college, but I wasn't. I was thinking about how I was going to tell my parents that I had lost my job, and now I was kicked out of high school. They gave me no other information, no direction, no guidance other than "there's the door, have a good one." And I don't quite remember how I told my parents, but I know it definitely wasn't a good time. But after the smoke cleared, I remember them telling me that I needed to go get my GED. So I went the next week and signed up to take the test at the local community college. They offered me classes and more schooling so that I might get a passing grade on the test. But I decided just to take a chance and go take the test straight out with no additional learning.

When I finally went to go take it, I passed on my first try at a 91 percent, which was pretty remarkable considering I never went to class. I definitely was not a dumb student and had a pretty high IQ and an ability to learn things when I paid attention. But I was dumb and reckless in my decision-making, and my thought process with day-to-day functions was not very good. I had no dreams, I had no aspirations, and I didn't believe in myself or have any vision. I was blind to a lot of things and so incredibly naive to say the least. The devil had a foothold on my life, and without total surrender and repentance to God, he was not gonna loosen his grip. The enemy was out to steal, kill, and destroy this young kid who was running from God. I had a calling on my life, and satan knew it and was not gonna ever let me attain it. So if he could start to destroy me at this early point in my life, I would never reach my full potential and could not be used by God. My parents were praying for me every single night, but I was careless and reckless with my decisions, and I was really falling away.

I received my GED right before my eighteenth birthday, and my parents sat me down and told me it was time to grow up, and I needed to go out and get a job. I was young, naive, and a little scared because I had no concept of hard work and discipline. I can remember getting in my car and driving around to go look for a job, and I ended up at some friends house who was a dropout too. This guy had more friends over who were also dropouts, and soon enough, I was going over there every single day. These guys were drug users and losers who had no goals or ambition in life, and they were gang members on top of all that. I was fascinated by these people because I had never seen anything like them ever in my life. I started going over there every single day and getting more and more involved with them. I was supposed to be out looking for work, but instead, I was hanging out and getting involved with these troubled kids who were also gang bangers. I can remember there were all kinds of them too;

they all lived in the same neighborhood. And all these young men had something in common, and that was no guidance and no fathers. These young thugs were from single-mother homes and had dropped out of school and turned to gangs. They were extremely violent, and all of them were drug users and thieves. And this is who I was somehow relating too, and these guys accepted me in their social circle. And why did they accept me in their circle? Because I had no dreams, no goals, and no aspirations just like them, and I had one thing no one else had...a car.

So we would drive around during the day and look for trouble, and trouble would somehow always find us. I would watch these guys get into fights with innocent people, and I hated it. But not enough to stop hanging around with them, I was still so fascinated, and I wanted to see more.

About this same time, someone from the church befriended me and tried to intervene and steer me in the right direction. His name was Pastor John Murillo, and he was a big guy and had an even bigger heart for the youth and the church. I was headed down the wrong way fast, and he was God-led, Spirit-filled, and was smart enough to see where I was going—nowhere. He befriended me and really tried to help by telling me I needed to give my life back to God and tried to get me involved with his youth ministry. At this same time, I was introduced to a recruiter from the US Marines, and he offered me a chance to get out of my small town and make something out of myself. I was really intrigued by this offer, and I was about to turn eighteen, so I accepted. This marine recruiter was in my face and relentless in his pursuit and offered me something I truly needed... discipline. But I was still caught up with these thugs and troublemakers and I was about to make the biggest mistake of my life.

One night, I was out with these guys, and they all decided they were gonna have a party and had me take them to go steal beer. They were successful, and we decided to find a house to drink at. One of my younger cousins was with us, and he said we could drink at his mom's house. Later that night, we were pretty intoxicated and got into a couple altercations with some college students. They stole our keg of beer that we had stolen, and a fight ensued, so we decided to follow them in my car and get our beer back. They were students at the local college, and reacting in anger, I jumped out of the car and broke their car window. I was gonna steal our keg back but then decided to steal everything they had. Almost immediately, I heard, "Freeze," and turned around to see four cops with guns drawn on me. I put my hands up, and they threw me on the ground and put me in handcuffs. They arrested my cousin who was also sitting in the car, waiting for me to get our beer back. He was later released with no reprimand, and I went to jail that night and was charged with a crime right before my eighteenth birthday. My chances of going to the marines were pretty much over and so were my chances of having any kind of a decent life.

I can remember that marine recruiter going to my court dates and pleading with the judge to defer the charges and let him take me to the service. But because it was a young college man, I had crossed, and I was a dumb Hispanic kid, I believe that judge had it in for me. He was going to teach me a lesson and make an example out of me and to any future car thieves. He said no and left me with the charge, and I was not able to enlist in the marines. I sat in jail for a couple of weeks and was released on probation. I knew I screwed up big, but I just seemed to blow it off and not let it affect me, which it should have. I was released from jail and went right back to hanging out with these thugs and robbers. I shaved my head just like them, and now I was one of them…a dropout, a thief, and a criminal. I had been to jail, and I thought I was tough now, and it basically legitimized me.

How sad and pathetic of a life I had at this moment. I had two parents who loved and cared for me and were praying for me at home while all this was happening. I had people trying to help me and pull me away from this wrong path; I was clearly headed down. I needed to repent at this moment and give my life back to God, but it was all pretty much lost at this point. I wanted acceptance at any price, and I wanted to fit in. Satan had full control of me now, and I had lost all my innocence and was guilty of so many atrocities. This time in my life is even hard to write. I've had to stop and pray and process these events as I'm sitting here in reflection. I feel so bad for my parents who had tried their best to provide for me and give me the best life they could. I let them down at this point, but everyone just kind of swept it under the rug and went on with their lives. They should have slapped the life out of me, beat me with a Bible, and locked me in my room. But I was eighteen, and they felt they couldn't do that anymore, and their prayers were the only answer. But I thank God for those prayers because it was only gonna get worse from here. I was gonna need God's mercy and protection even more from this point on.

CHAPTER 3

Lawless and Hopeless

I was eighteen years old and desperate to find myself in a world that was failing me to a point of no return. One of my cousins had introduced me to rap music, and it opened my mind to a dark world that I never even knew existed but one I wanted to live in. In this world, you drank and smoked weed, had beautiful women on your arm, and would do anything it took to be legit. A dropout and newly appointed malefactor, I rode with thugs, and these wannabe gangsters and was out to wreak mayhem and havoc on society. Every single night was a party and a quest to get blackout drunk or get high on weed and anything else you could get your hands on. These guys would go out and rob people in the day time and trade their loot for money to buy drugs and liquor by nightfall.

My family pretty much just let me do what I wanted at this point. I was eighteen and a big disappointment to them all. I still saw my grandparents from time to time, and I'm sure they were worried about me and where I was headed in life. But all of this was the least of my worries because I had a new mission…to be absolutely nothing. I had no goals, no dreams…nothing but listening to this dark and vile rap music and meeting easy, loose women. I went to hood parties with these guys and would see the prettiest girl there and would walk up and start talking to her.

Before anyone knew, we would be driving around, making out in my car, and pulling over at a park somewhere to have sex. I started accumulating multiple girlfriends and would always have two or three girls on my arm. We would go out to these parties and get drunk and get high and live life like there was no tomorrow. I didn't care about anything except being accepted and being legit. I idolized these rappers in the rap songs I listened to and wanted to be exactly like them. They were womanizers who did drugs and drank and talked about violence and even murder. My favorite rapper at the time was Tupac Shakur, and I wanted to be exactly like him and modeled myself after him every chance I could. The women loved him, and the gangsters and thugs respected him, and he was a mega star at the time. The women liked me, and I had them around me like I was the star, but I knew it was because I was the only guy with a car, but I didn't care. I was living my young life to the fullest, and I was not worried about tomorrow or having any kind of future because I couldn't see one. I was fascinated by these young gang members because they didn't care about rules, the law, or what anyone thought of them. They were all fighters and thugs who carried knives, guns, and various other weapons of the sort. They were violent and were from broken families, and nobody loved them or cared for them. But I was nonviolent, and I had people that loved me and who were praying for me, so there was a big difference. But these guys offered me acceptance in a world where I felt I didn't fit in, and I did with these guys.

When I was younger, I can remember riding my bike around the really nice neighborhood my parents had moved into. I can remember seeing all these young white families with their children, and I was awestruck. They were really nice-looking couples, God-fearing with good jobs, and went to church on Sunday mornings. I was around nine years old at the time, and I can remember trying to envision myself with a wife and kids and living in a nice home, and for some reason, I couldn't. I must have felt I wasn't good enough at the time, and I couldn't imagine a woman loving me or even liking me. I had no vision for myself, no drive, no dreams or aspirations, and that was still true at eighteen. I had messed up high school, I wanted to be a marine, and I had messed that up. So I felt there was no hope for me as I downed bottles of liquor and had one-night stands with every woman I felt attracted to. I was getting arrested every month for one thing or another. I was on probation, and I was failing UAs left and right. Every stint I did in jail, I would always work out and hit the weights. I would get in great shape, come out bigger and more legitimized every single time. My Christian faith was just a thing of the past now, and I was destined for prison and ultimately hell.

We would go out every night looking for trouble and fights and talk to every female that crossed our paths. One night, one of the guys suggested we go to a nearby city where he supposedly knew some pretty women there. So we all packed in my black firebird and took the twenty-minute drive to the next town over. We were getting drunk, listening to music when we pulled up to a ratty broken-down trailer park. And instead of a bunch of women like my buddy said, we sat there and waited, and one young woman came out.

This brown-skinned, brown-eyed girl walked up and said hi. The first thing I noticed was her dark curly hair and her big bright smile. I was immediately awestruck as I introduced myself. Our eyes locked, and I believe it was infatuation at first sight. This young lady came from a broken family, she was raised by her mom and stepfather, and she never knew her real dad. She had two other sisters all one year apart, and she was the prettiest out of her siblings. I can't recall exactly how it all went down after that, but soon I was driving over there every single night to go see her. She was fifteen about to be sixteen, and I was already eighteen years old and I had to ask for permission to date her. I was calling her my girlfriend after just a few short weeks, and soon enough we were having a sexual relationship. We were both young and in love with each other and couldn't get enough of one another. She was introduced to my family, and I was so proud of her because of her beauty, but other than that, she had nothing really going for her. And I had nothing going for me either. I didn't know how to work or do anything for myself. But the attraction between us was undeniable, and I couldn't get enough of her. What I didn't realize was that she came from a lot of hurt and abuse from her mom and stepfather. Her stepdad was a Mexican national from Mexico and a drug dealer for the cartel. Her mother was into witchcraft and black magic, and both were people that any person with half a brain cell wouldn't want anything to do with. Her mom liked me for the most part, and her dad just kind of acknowledged me when he had too. This man sold cocaine and was a "do as I say, not as I do" kind of guy. He had made sexual advances on his step-daughter in the past, and that was something she had confided in me with, and it really hurt her deeply.

Her real father never knew her or even made an attempt to know her, and that was something she was still trying to overcome. She was looking for love in all the wrong ways, and she had been mistreated and abused in her youth. It was very sad, and when she had told me all this, I felt very bad for her and even told her I would never hurt her in any way. And it would seem that a good story could come out of all this. I could be the right person she needed to over-come all these dark secrets and hurts. I could love her in the right way and help her heal from all the brokenness and open wounds from her past. But this was me we're talking about, Mr. Womanizer running from God and fully controlled by satan, undisciplined and not a whole lot of respect for the lost women I was meeting and befriend-ing. I was full of pride and low self-esteem, and I was very selfish and carried a lot of hurt with me. Maybe from the past with my father or maybe from the kids that used to pick on me in school? But I was not man enough or emotionally stable enough to handle any kind of serious relationship.

Soon enough she was head over heels in love with me, and I was head over heels in love and lust with her. She became a desirable object to me; she was only sixteen and searching for that love her real father never gave her. I took advantage of that, and I used it for my own selfish desires. We were too young to be doing the things we were doing. We would go out and get drunk together, and sometimes we would get into arguments and fights. But we would make up and carry on like nothing happened, and that continued for months. At first, I was faithful and tried my best to be good to her, but one night, that all changed. She had told me in not so many audible words that she had cheated on me, or at least that's what I had come to believe. It took me by surprise at first, and then I can remember real anger and eventually an outburst. I grabbed her upset screaming at her, and she turned around and punched me in the face and ran out of my vehicle. She was a tough girl and a fighter, and that made me even more mad but made the attraction even stronger. We eventually made up, and she forgave me, and I forgave her, but now we were a certified dysfunctional couple.

A few seasons passed, and it was now the winter of ninety-six when she had sat me down and told me the news. She was excited but very nervous when she told me she thought she was pregnant. I can remember the shock and how scared I felt about this, and I can recall us having to tell her mom and stepfather. It wasn't the happiest of moments having to tell them, but we did it and had gotten through it. They were not very happy whatsoever, but what else could they really do or say? Their daughter was going to have to finish high school pregnant and be a young teen mother. And they told me that I had better get a job and a place for her because she couldn't stay with them anymore. So basically that was that, I was going to be a young father. I was nineteen years old, and she was just shy of seventeen when this all happened, and our lives would be changed forever.

The next nine months were not gonna be very easy on either of us, and I tried to do my best as a soon-to-be father. But the hurt and anger I felt toward her just grew to resentment because I was scared of responsibility. And my low self-esteem and insecurities kept getting in the way of us having any kind of decent relationship. We both had never been parents before, and I'm sure she was scared to death too. I would get mad at her and would become abusive toward her verbally and mentally. I was not a tough guy, but I wanted her to respect me, and I thought scaring her would get that respect. But all I came off as was a douchebag who needed to be taught a serious lesson about respecting women. She kept all this from her parents because she knew what they would do if they found out.

One night at her parents' home, I found one of her stepfather's guns and decided I was gonna take it. I wanted to go out and shoot it, and then somehow I decided to never give it back. I was working and trying to figure out how I was gonna get her and myself a place to live. Some of our fights had gotten so bad people had pulled over and asked if we were okay because we would be arguing somewhere. I was young and naive about the world and really scared to say the least. This was a time I should have been in college, getting an education and planning my future career. But no one ever told me about college or asked me what my plans were for my future. I came from a home where both my parents worked their butts off to give me something in life, but they never went past high school. So they couldn't tell me about something they knew nothing about. They were very supportive of me and her and gave us their full blessing to give them a grandchild. But I needed some serious help in life, and I wasn't getting it. I really needed God.

But now I was carrying a firearm that I stole from my girlfriend's stepdad who worked for the Mexican drug cartel. And every decision I was making from here on out was all bad and not very smart. I was going out to hood parties and, of course, getting drunk and talking to women while my pregnant girlfriend was at home, waiting for me. I would get drunk and then pull out the pistol and show everybody. We would go out to the fields, and all my thug buddies would take turns shooting it. And of course, with this gun, I was getting respect, and nobody would cross me or say a negative word to me, and I liked that. I was careless with it, and a couple times, I used it to shoot in the air to scare off some of my naysayers. I should have been home with Sofia and going to work every day, but instead, I was out being an idiot. But I did finally manage to get us an apartment right before she was about to be due. I don't really remember how I received the money, but let's just say it probably wasn't legal. But I knew what her parents had said, and I took that as seriously as I possibly could and had rented us a small place.

I did the best I knew how to provide a place for us and buy baby furniture, a television, and a bed for us to sleep. I resented Sofia for putting all this responsibility on me that I knew I wasn't ready for, and I couldn't handle. She was nine months pregnant, and I had already put her through hell with the cheating and all the arguments. I was abusive to her mentally and a couple times came close to being physical. She would accuse me of cheating on her all the time, and I would get so mad and yell at her because I knew it was true. My poor baby who was in her womb, I believe God protected her from all the nonsense that was going on outside. I was a complete monster, ugly, evil, vile, and angry at the world. My anger and resentment toward Sofia grew and grew, and I would go out with my friends and not come home till the morning. My dad finally intervened and helped me get a job with one of his oilfield buddies, and I started working right before she was going to give birth.

I straightened up for a little while and stopped going out with my thug friends and tried to focus on Sofia and the upcoming birth of our child. I decided to be respectful to her and our unborn baby, and I decided I had to work to keep a roof over our heads. I was scared of becoming a father, and I didn't really know what to expect. Some counseling and classes would have come in very handy around this time, but I didn't have that luxury. It was hard, but I knew it was time to man up and take care of my responsibilities. I was trying the best I could at the time, but I really needed some direction on what to do next as a soon to be father. I write this part of my story in regret and embarrassment, not a high point of my life whatsoever, but it all happened. I was young and didn't understand the important things in life. Like being true to someone and being true to myself, I was not a good boyfriend and not a good person. I was lost to the world, and there was no coming back, and so my story goes on.

Sofia was really glowing at nine months prego, and I can remember her pretty brown skin and how beautiful she looked. I had somehow managed to buy her an engagement ring and asked her to marry me. She immediately said yes with tears in her eyes, and we hugged and kissed each other, and it was a very nice moment. I was trying to do the right thing and do what my parents expected me to do. But I knew deep down in my heart that I wasn't ready to be married and settle down. I had just turned twenty, and I had a long way to go. We had bought everything we needed for the baby, and we were ready and waiting. We were deciding on baby names when the name Jocelyn had caught my attention and just stuck. And if it was a boy, I figured Jason was a good name as any, and that was that. We were excited, and my family was very excited. I can remember being really anxious and very happy.

It was a long summer for the both of us, but at the end of August, she finally had gone into labor, and I can remember how nervous I was. Her family had taken her to the hospital, and they called me and told me she was in labor and to hurry. I raced over and was by Sofia's side the entire time as were her family. My family showed up, and they were very excited about the birth of their grandchild. Both of our families were really supportive. She was in labor for a whole night and into the next day, and it was not an easy time. But that day, she gave birth to our child, and it was a beautiful little baby girl. I can remember looking at her in amazement, and I could not believe she was actually mine. I can also remember holding her for the first time and how excited and happy I was to have her in my life. I couldn't believe someone like me could have had a hand in making this beautiful little girl. I remember my father kissing Sofia on the forehead and telling her thank you. My mother and sister were elated. It was the highlight in my otherwise broken life, and I'm sure it was the same for Sofia. I was a father of this little girl, and my life was gonna change forever, and I knew it. We named her Jocelyn Rebecca. And she was the prettiest little baby in the whole wide world, and I can still remember telling God thank you.

CHAPTER 4

The Children

Now my life had suddenly changed for the better, and I was a father of a beautiful baby girl who looked just like me. She was born healthy and happy, and she was definitely a light to my otherwise dark world. I tried my best to straighten up and be a good father to my newborn little girl, but I was so scared at the same time.

Sofia and I were engaged and had a small two-bedroom apartment together. I was working and trying to become a man and trying to take care of my new family. I wasn't going out with my buddies anymore, and I was definitely trying my best to be faithful. But I was angry at Sofia for whatever reason, and I started treating her bad because I hated myself. We were getting into arguments, and I was trying my best to be responsible, but the anger kept building and building. This was definitely a time I needed God in my life, but I was so far gone from serving him, and there was no way back. I could feel the weight of the world on my shoulders, and I felt like I was losing everything I wanted at the time like my freedom and my careless lifestyle I had grown accustomed to. But I knew I had parents expecting me to do the right thing and a father-in-law in the Mexican drug cartel expecting me to do the same. I also had his gun that I had taken from him months earlier that I kept on me at all times. I hung out with some rough characters, and I knew I needed extra protection just in case something went wrong. I had made a lot of enemies, and I thought they could come for me at any given moment. I held a lot of emotions in because I hated confrontation in all forms. And I hated fighting with Sofia, and I knew what she and everyone else expected from me. To be a responsible father, to work and take care of this little child who was helpless at this moment. The enemy had a strong grip on my life at the time, and satan wanted me dead, and deep down I knew it.

A couple of months into our new life and arrangement, Sofia and I had gotten into a really bad argument, and it became physical. She hit me with a pan, and I hit her in the face with a closed fist and caused her forehead to bleed. I felt so bad because she immediately began to cry and ran upstairs to the bedroom. I started freaking out, and I knew I did something very wrong and cowardly. Who was I? What had I become in this world that I would even react to someone like this? I had an anger toward women that was built up inside me, and it came out in the worst possible way. I was not raised in an abusive home or had any kind of abuse given to me that would give me any kind of excuse for this. I was just angry at Sofia for taking my young, free life away and making me have to man up and be a father. But I loved my little girl, and now she was locked in the room with Sofia. I immediately ran to the door and told her I was sorry, and I wouldn't do it again. I felt so bad. But she was already on the phone with her mother and stepfather, and I could hear her telling them to come pick her up. I knew her stepdad was a bad man, and the consequences were gonna be severe. But before I could make my escape, they were coming through the front door, screaming and in total astonishment. I panicked and didn't know what to expect or do; they came in and walked right past me and took their daughter and my daughter with them. The next thing I knew, I was grabbing my father-in-law's gun and started grabbing my clothes. I was gonna leave the apartment and go somewhere else...anywhere else except where I was at. But when I went to the front door, I could hear cops and lots of them. I glanced out the window and saw a whole task force.

Sofia's mother had called the police and had told them that I had assaulted their daughter and was armed. I guess Sofia had told her mom that I had taken her stepfather's pistol, and it was loaded. They started pounding on the door, telling me to come out with my hands up. I was really scared and confused, and there was no way I was gonna walk out that door with a loaded firearm. When I looked out the window, I saw the SWAT team and every cop in the city outside. They were speaking over a speakerphone, telling me to give myself up or they were gonna open fire. I looked out the window again to see the local news agency and multiple reporters with cameras. I was so scared, and all this escalated from my poor decision-making and abusive behavior. They knocked again, but this time, with a battering ram, and it was loud. It was time to go. I did not want to go to jail, and my options were extremely limited. I ran upstairs and locked myself in the back bedroom. *Boom!* I heard the front door explode into the house like a bomb. I could hear police and SWAT storming through the apartment and up the stairs. I opened the back window, expecting to have more cops and SWAT surrounding me, but there was nothing. No one was back there. I grabbed my gun and jumped out the window, falling two stories to the bottom, and did a tuck-in roll. I could hear the police canines barking and running to the back-yard. I immediately jumped over the back fence and onto the high-way and oncoming traffic. I ran and ran and ran until I could find a payphone to call my buddy to come and pick me up. I was on the run and was wanted by the local police, and I had a gun on me, and I knew none of this was going to end well.

I decided to toss the gun in a dumpster, but I thought a kid or somebody could potentially find it and accidentally shoot them-selves. So I buried it in the dirt next to a mini-mart and took off with my friend to go somewhere and hide. The next day, I was on the front page of the local newspaper as a wanted man, and they reported that I was armed and dangerous. I couldn't believe that my life had come to this, and I was in so much trouble. I went to see my parents, and they told me to turn myself in. I agreed and left back to my buddies' house where I was hiding out. The next night, his wife decided she was gonna turn me in as I was sleeping in the downstairs basement. I awoke to cops walking around upstairs and could hear her telling them I was in the substructure below. I took off once again out the back window running, and I never looked back.

About a week had passed, and I hadn't spoken to Sofia or seen my daughter, and I missed them very much. I knew the right thing to do was to turn myself in, I had promised my parents, and they were expecting me to do the right thing. My dad drove me down to the police station, and the cops arrested me for assault and domestic violence. I was worried about someone finding that handgun and shooting themselves, so I told the police where it could be found. They told me I did the right thing by turning it in, and they would tell the judge. The next couple of weeks, I sat in jail, but I was bonded out to fight my case. I was in a lot of trouble, and I wasn't going to take their bad deal and end up in jail for the next two years. So I figured I would fight it until they offered me something that wouldn't ruin my life more than I already had. It had been months since I had seen Sofia and our daughter Jocelyn, and I missed them. I would try to call, but her parents would block me and threaten me with the police. I kept going to court and so did Sofia and her mother who was trying to make sure I was convicted. But after a while, Sofia and I started talking again, and I apologized for what I had done to her, and she forgave me. She started sneaking off to see me, and I was able to see our daughter. I loved my little girl, and I just wanted this whole mess to go away, but it wasn't going to.

One day, I decided to go see my little girl who was almost a year old because Sofia had said her parents were not there, and I could come by. I had my buddies drive me to her trailer home, and I was excited to see my daughter and just give her a hug and say hello. My friends waited in the car as I went to go knock on Sofia's door and see my kid. She brought Jocelyn out, and I was so happy to hug her and give her a kiss. We had been through so much and I was just so grateful. We were having a nice little visit when all of a sudden, her parents drove up. Her mom got out of the car and went inside while her stepdad just stared at me evilly and left. Sofia told me to leave too, and I said okay, but while I was still holding my daughter, another car drove up. I turned around and saw one guy pointing a gun at my buddies as they put their car in reverse and took off, leaving me. I gave my daughter to Sofia, and her mom grabbed her and my child and locked them inside their trailer home. I was stuck with no car and no friends as these guys walked toward me, and I knew they were only there for me. They were all gang members, and all of them had no expression on their faces and were all drugged out. They worked for my girlfriend's father who was their supplier and they were paid with narcotics to teach me a lesson. I tried to escape by jumping over a fence, but they grabbed me and started beating me with fist. All of them took turns hitting me and pistol-whipped me until I was unconscious, then for whatever reason, they stopped and ran away. At the exact same time this was happening, my mother was in church, and the women there were praying. The Holy Spirit had told Sr. Janie Ramos that someone in a trailer park needed prayer, and all the women immediately started praying for this person. My mother said she and my aunt Marlene knew in their hearts that it was me and asked God to protect me.

When I had finally woken up, I walked to a neighbor's house down the road and called my dad for a ride. I was bleeding from my head, and my teeth were broken and bleeding. I had black eyes, and my face swelled up to the size of a watermelon, and I didn't know where I was. My ribs were broken, and they had stomped on my feet and legs; I was in total pain. I couldn't remember my name or what I was doing, but the neighbors had given my dad directions. I knew I screwed up, and I knew I deserved what had been done to me in retaliation for my abusive actions. But I was not gonna give up on being a father to my daughter, and so I slowly healed over the next three months, and life went on.

Sofia and I eventually reconciled, and she left her parents, and we moved back in together and tried to make things work again. My daughter was just two years old when Sofia gave birth to our son, and I was so happy to have him in my life. We named him Noah Marcus, and he looked just like his mother, and I was happy to have a boy. Where it was easy being a father to a little girl, it was harder for me to be father to him. He was a happy little boy and very handsome. His dark eyes and thick eyebrows made him very striking. I started leaving Sofia home with our two kids and taking off with my buddies to go drink and party again. I was not a good father to the two babies that I had at home waiting for me. I was out being an immature jerk and talking to other women every chance I could, and I knew it was wrong, but I didn't care. Sofia was faithful, and she had no other choice because she was busy being a mother to our two children. And she was a good mom, and I knew that I was lucky to have her in my life and as the mother of my children. If I could go back in time, I would spend every moment with those three people and never take them for granted. But life doesn't give you second chances, and that's why you have to do your best every day and treat people with respect every day. But I was caught up with my thug friends and the party life, and I treated my family so wrong. I eventually got caught up with the law again and ended up doing some major jail time. I was in and out of jail while my children were learning to walk and learning to read without their father present. I lost out on so much that even today, it's hard for me to accept, and I've had to ask God to forgive me and help me get pass these regrets.

I was constantly being unfaithful and disrespecting Sofia, and she finally started to get fed up with all my inconsistencies and short-comings. I couldn't keep a job, and I was not supporting her or my children like I should have been. I was in and out of jail so much that she started to look elsewhere for someone who could love her properly. My kids were well taken care of, but they needed a father in their life and a father's security. I didn't offer any of that, and I was so caught up in my sin that I couldn't see anything but that. I was seeing another female behind Sofia's back, and this girl started to tell people she was pregnant from me. I was locked up again when Sofia finally said enough was enough and finally ended our relationship. It was devastating to me because I loved my children, but I knew deep down in my heart that I didn't love Sofia. Not the way she needed to be loved because with Sofia, to be extremely honest, it was just lust. I never gave us a chance to ever be in love because I never had gotten to know her, and she never really had known me. We were together for a total of six years when we split, and I didn't blame her for it one bit. I was sitting in a halfway house, doing a two-year sentence for writing bad checks when Sofia and I were first together, and she was pregnant with Jocelyn. All that stuff I had bought for us in the beginning was purchased with bad checks that eventually all bounced. So I was charged years later and had to serve time in a halfway house. The Lord was still protecting me even though I was running from him and his calling because all the trouble I was in, I never went to prison. God's mercy and grace was always somehow covering me, but I was too dumb to realize it.

I had gotten a phone call from Sofia, and she had told me she found out about the girl I was messing with, and someone had told her that she was pregnant. She told me she couldn't deal with the abusive behaviors and my infidelities, and she was leaving. I told her I was sorry for what I had done to her, but I understood that it was time to let her go. I was getting caught for my crimes and the wrongs I was doing to her and my children. My daughter was five years old now, and she was the most beautiful little girl I had ever known. I remember Sofia and I fought so much in front of her that my little girl had gotten tired of it. She must have been four years old at the time, and her mother and I were in such turmoil. She grabbed Sofia's hand, and she grabbed my hand and put the two of them together.

She yelled out, "Stop fighting and be nice!"

It just broke my heart to pieces. I was uncontrollable, but she had put me in my place. My son Noah was just three years old when Sofia and I called it quits, and it hurt my heart so bad. He was a beautiful boy who had been blessed with his mother's good looks. I was so proud to have such a good little boy. He was a happy kid and always smiling, and it broke my heart to think I was never a good father to him. But I knew it was over, and I knew I had treated Sofia so badly the whole relationship. I wanted her to be happy, and I knew she deserved much more than what I had given her and that was it. She had brought the kids to come see me a couple of times, and I was happy with that.

When Sofia was first pregnant with our little girl, I had found out that there was another little girl that I thought maybe was mine. But I never was able to find out for sure, and I had gone to see her a couple of times, but the grandmother told me to leave them alone, so I did. And this new woman who had accused me of getting her pregnant was a local town runaround and was seeing multiple men. She blamed me for the pregnancy, and it was the nail in the coffin with my relationship with Sofia. I was locked up when all this had occurred, so basically I couldn't confirm or deny that this was my child. That woman gave birth to a little boy and gave him up for adoption at birth. A very sad ending to a ridiculous life and sexual escapades that ended sadly and disastrous. I was careless with my life and with who I slept with. I didn't follow God's laws or any laws for that matter, and it had all caught up with me.

While all this was happening, I started to believe there was not a God, and that he didn't exist. How could he? I just had started to believe that maybe Christianity was just a lie to scare us into being compliant. I didn't even believe in myself anymore, and now I was believing that there wasn't even a God at all. I was twenty-four about to be twenty-five and thought I knew everything, but that was a big lie on my part. I knew nothing about life at this point; all I knew was that I was in deep turmoil, and I was not gonna let it set me back any longer. I was gonna get it all back somehow, I wanted a new life, I knew my old life was done, and it was time to start over.

While I was still locked up in the halfway house, I had gotten an overnight pass to go home and spend time with my family. But instead I snuck off to a nightclub in another town to meet women and get drunk. I was walking through the crowded club and enjoying my night out alone when I saw something that took me by surprise. Standing across the club was this pretty dark-haired woman with light skin. She was very different from anyone I had ever seen before and was dancing by herself with a drink in her hand. I was nervous, and my heart was pounding, but I was totally awestruck, and I had to say hello. Something inside me had never felt this way before, and I knew this woman was different. We had shared a moment, and she gave me a kiss at the end of the night, but she had a boyfriend with whom she was fighting with. I was at the end of my relationship with Sofia, and of course, I was already looking for redemption. She was basically being unfaithful to her boyfriend, and Sofia was still fresh on my mind and still in my heart. We parted ways that night, and I figured I would never see her again. But I ran into her three months later when I went to the doctor's office, and I was elated. She was the receptionist, and I couldn't stop staring at her, and my heart was pounding so hard. I told her hello, and we smiled at each other, and boy, my heart felt like it skipped a beat. There was something really special about her, and I just couldn't figure it out. She was the female version of me maybe? Maybe it was love at first sight. I don't know, but my life didn't feel so bad anymore now that I knew that she existed. Her name was Mary.

I went on with my life and was released from the halfway house finally. I left on foot with no car and a bag of clothes. That's all I owned after Sofia and I had finally split, but I was just so happy to finally be a free man. I was free from both a relationship and from being locked up, and I wanted to party and have a good time. I moved back home with my parents and had gotten a job at the local slaughterhouse. I bought myself some new clothes and a car, and I started going out every single night and meeting new people and plenty of pretty women that I was befriending. I would see my kids as often as I could and would take them to go eat or to the park to play. I loved them so much, and they were always so excited to see me, and when they would see me, they would always yell, "Daddy!" and run to me and give me a big hug. They meant everything to me, and Jocelyn and Noah were the only good thing I had at this point in my life. They were amazing beautiful kids, and I was proud that they were mine.

Sofia had met another man who was in the service and had moved on with her life. I was happy for her and just wanted her to find peace and happiness with someone. I was an undisciplined immature train wreck who was running from a mighty God who still loved me, even though obviously at the time, I didn't love him. I was twenty-five years old and into rap music and loose women. I failed at being a good father, but I loved my two children, and even though I had lost everything, I was resilient, and I got back up. I was in good shape physically, but I had a lot of growing up to do mentally.

One summer day, I had received a phone call at my parent's home. I answered it, and it was Mary. I was so excited, and I had the biggest smile on my face. She had gotten my number from the doctor's office where she worked. She said she was finally single and wanted to go have a drink and talk. I was elated. I felt like life maybe could be good again.

CHAPTER 5

Something about Mary

Mary and I met up for a drink one August evening, and we talked for what must have been a good couple of hours. She was the most beautiful woman I had ever seen in my life, and of course, I immediately needed to tell her that. She was really pretty but very quiet and withdrawn, and I was instantly intrigued by her beauty and her shyness. She had just gotten out of a bad relationship with her ex-boyfriend, and she was not looking for anything serious. And either was I, but she was everything I dreamed of in a woman as far as looks were concerned, and I was very infatuated. We kept on seeing each other, and I stopped going out with all the other women I was seeing at the time.

Mary, at this time, loved going out drinking and dancing, and that's what we did. She liked being single and wanted to meet new people, but I wasn't too keen on that idea. I liked her a lot, and that was all that mattered. I had always gotten what I wanted, but she was not gonna be that easy. She had met my children, and we would take them to go eat and do fun things together, and I appreciated that. I knew in my heart that this woman was everything I ever wanted, but she was very hesitant with me. She came from a poor family and was raised by her parents with nine other siblings. Her parents were still married, but they lived in Mexico, and this young woman was left here to take care of herself. She was twenty-three at this time, and

I was twenty-five years old, and both of us were very different but also very much the same. Her ex-boyfriends never treated her right, and she was very shy, and she had been through a whole lot. She was into drugs and the party scene, all these bad habits she had picked up from her ex-boyfriends. She was young and a free spirit, and she didn't really talk a lot or express herself or her desires. But I had good intentions with her, and we always enjoyed our time together. I was very insecure, and I felt like everybody wanted her, and I was very jealous if she talked to anybody or interacted with someone else. She would get a lot of attention when we would go out, and she really liked that, and so did I, but I was always uneasy.

After about two months of dating, I had moved into a new apartment. We continued going out together, and I had asked her to move in with me. By this time, I was totally in love with this woman, and she was still enjoying her young life and having a good time. But she agreed and showed up with all her stuff one day, which wasn't much, but I didn't have much either. And we started becoming really close and became very fond of each other very fast, but it was not gonna be easy.

Sofia was now engaged and was about to marry her high school sweetheart, and she called one day with some shocking news. Her and her soon-to-be new husband, who was in the service, were moving to California and taking my children. I was so devastated by this, and I knew there was nothing I could really do to stop it from happening. I took it pretty hard because I loved my children very much, and I was gonna miss them.

Around the same time, Mary's very jealous sister had told me that Mary was seeing other guys and wasn't "down for me." I took that news very seriously and hard, and I felt like my world was falling apart. After a couple of arguments and fights, we had gotten through it, but it started to change my feelings toward Mary. It brought out some hurt and anger that I hadn't felt in a very long time, and I didn't want that to happen with her. I decided I was gonna break things off with Mary, and I had called her to tell her it was over. But she had some news to tell me, and I was not ready for what she was about to say. I was still mad about the things her sister had told me, but when I started to bring it up, Mary told me she was pregnant.

This news took me by surprise, and my heart was torn about everything that was going on, but I needed to grow up and be a man now. I told her we could make things work, and I was not gonna leave her side, and deep down, I was actually kind of happy. I liked Mary a lot, and it was time for me to be mature and take responsibility for my actions and be a father once again. Sofia had remarried and brought my kids over so they could tell me goodbye. I cried and cried and cried and kissed Jocelyn and Noah goodbye. It was the hardest moment of my young life because I wasn't sure that I would ever get to see them again. And now Mary was pregnant with my third child, and my life was changing drastically. Mary was a party girl who liked illicit drugs and alcohol so her being pregnant made me a little nervous. We had drank and partied and had a good time together, but now she was pregnant, and she was really scared. But I had been through this before, and I wasn't scared at all. My mom and dad had met Mary, and they liked her and gave us their blessing and told us they were praying for us. My dad gave me a job working for him, and I started working on a drilling rig, making really good money. Mary was still working as a receptionist at a doctor's office, and she took this pregnancy seriously. I watched her go from a party girl who liked to drink and go dancing change into a responsible soon-to-be mother.

My life was changing drastically, and I was not sure how to handle it properly, but I was working really hard, and I was determined to do the right thing. I would do anything for Mary, and I was totally in love with this woman. Sure, we had a shaky start with both of us coming from bad relationships, but we were both good people. I saw her for who she really was…a shy girl who didn't know how to express herself properly or her feelings. She put her trust in me, and I had a chance to really do something different with my life—be a good man finally to someone who needed me, and I was gonna do that.

My children were now two thousand miles away, and I was very sad and a little depressed. But at the same time, I was excited for

Mary and I and our upcoming child, and I believe she was also. I wanted to marry her and make her my wife, and I told her that every day and all the time. She had a hard time trusting people because she had been hurt so many times before, and I completely understood that. And it was hard for me to let go of all the women I knew and had befriended when I was single, but somehow I did. And so we should have been able to start a new successful relationship and a new life together…but no, that did not happen.

I was working really long hours on a drilling rig that my dad was also working on, and he was one of the bosses. He saw that I needed some discipline and hard work because, of course, I was about to have another child. So he gave me a big break by putting me to work for his drilling company, and I really appreciated that and the big paychecks it brought. Mary was a couple of months pregnant, and she was starting to show her little baby bump. I would talk to my kids on the phone every week, and I really missed them. You would think, *Man, this guy got a second chance and was finally gonna have a great life*…but no. You see I was still mad at Mary for seeing other men when we were first dating. And I was running from God, and satan had full control of my life because I would not give my heart back to the Lord.

One day, I was working on the rig, and a guy who my dad had just hired came out and tried to befriend me. He seemed like a cool guy, and I wasn't doing anything wrong but watching the rig because it was shut down for the day. So I was out there by myself and just thinking about my life and my kids who I was missing. He started telling me about this drug that he did, and it was like hard white crystals that you could snort or smoke. I knew nothing about hard drugs, but I knew Mary had done this drug before, so I kept listening. He told me he had some and wanted to know if I wanted to try it. So stupidly, I said yeah, and he pulled out a bag and a pipe, and we started smoking it. I immediately felt wide awake, and I felt invincible, and I had never felt this way before. It made me feel energetic and happy, and it made me forget about all my stress and the fact my kids were gone. I wish I never had said yes to that drug; I had never known addiction or had ever tried drugs like this. But I liked the feeling of numbness I had all of a sudden to this broken life that I was so adamantly trying to fix.

I came home that night and spent the evening with my pregnant girlfriend, and I was happy and didn't care or was worried about anything. I was with Mary that night, and she had no idea I was on drugs, and it felt euphoric. I was immediately addicted to this feeling, and I couldn't wait to do drugs again. And I did it again and again because this guy who was working for my dad was now my new drug dealer. My life felt great…this drug made me forget all my problems, and I was able to work long hours and go home and be with my girlfriend. I was making money and lots of it because I was working seven days a week with only one day off. And this stuff kept me going and going, and it was really a pleasurable experience to me, Mary eventually started to notice that I was on something. But I was working and doing what I was supposed to do at the time, so she didn't complain at first. This drug was an evil drug that I now know came from the pits of hell and something satan brought to this world. I was in good shape, and this young woman thought I was very handsome, so I believe I was able to get away with it. I shouldn't have ever tried drugs because I was opening doors that I wouldn't be able to close. Drugs are not the answer to this life God has given us. In fact, it's a tool the devil uses to destroy us. Drugs are not the answer to pain, and they should never be tried at any cost…just say no! But it's hard because we're broken inside, and we need Jesus, and our souls are crying out for the Holy Spirit. And when we don't answer that call in the right way (with God), we as humans tend to answer it with drugs and alcohol. And that's exactly what I did. I filled my broken heart which needed Jesus…with illicit drugs. And I became very addicted very fast because I needed God inside my heart. But instead I opened demonic doors, and the devil came through to steal, kill, and destroy my life. Once again, I needed the salvation of Jesus Christ in my broken heart, but I instead I chose this.

Mary was close to her due date and was going to work every day, coming home, and going to bed every night by ten. And I was working crazy hours, days and nights, and my schedule was always changing because I worked a swing shift. And I was buying this drug from this guy on my crew who had gotten me to initially try it. Then I met other people who were selling it, and I started buying it from them also. The next thing I knew, all this money I was making was going right to these guys to feed my habit. I was doing this drug at work, and I was doing it at home in my bathroom and in the living room when Mary was asleep. I started to watch pornography, and the addiction to that really started to take hold. Mary was pregnant and always tired, and I didn't want to bother or wake her. So I would stay up all night, smoking this drug and watching porn, and I truly became addicted to this upside-down lifestyle.

My behavior was abusive and inexcusable to say the very least…I was slowly becoming a monster as this drug took control of my mind. One night, Mary was sleeping in the bedroom while I was getting high in the next room alone. She told me she awoke to a nine-foot black demon standing next to her bed in the middle of night. She said she was so scared, and she wanted to go get me, but she couldn't because she knew I was getting high in the next room. She prayed to God and asked him to help her and rebuked the demon, and it fled. I feel so bad today as I reflect on this true story of a broken life, a life that I had created. But I also was negatively affecting other people's lives and using things that had been done to me as an excuse to do whatever I wanted.

Mary was trying her best to give our upcoming child a chance to live, and all I was doing was being selfish and evil. Satan had full control of me, and God was just a memory of a past that I no longer wanted or cared about. Mary didn't fight or argue with me because at this point, she just let me do what I wanted because she knew it was pointless. Being so close to her due date, she had to finally quit her day job, and I was now supporting her financially. I was high on drugs every single day, and Mary just let me do what I needed to do. These dealers were making money off me and were selling me drugs every single chance they could. I don't even know how I functioned or made it to work; I would be up for three or four days at a time and would still go in every day. I put everyone around me in danger by going to work high with no sleep. This addiction was a generational curse passed down from my grandfather who was a drinker to my father who was an addict. But I would never blame them because they always treated me well and gave me a good childhood. This was something that was passed down spiritually but was something I had to say yes too and accept, and I would not be able to beat this addiction by myself. It would not be that easy.

Mary finally went into labor and gave birth to a beautiful baby boy, we named him Jonah Thomas, and I was really happy. I was full on in my addiction, and I can remember barely making it to the hospital...high out of my mind. He was so beautiful, and I just knew I was gonna have to straighten up my life when he eventually came home. Mary looked so beautiful holding my son...this woman that I had fallen in love with and I cared so much about. But I had fallen into drugs and was getting high and working so much that I couldn't feel anything anymore. I was numb to the world and everything in it because of this crap I was smoking. It was euphoric to me, and I just could not stop doing it to save my life. She brought our son home, and I tried to quit, but after a couple weeks, I started doing it again. I was really unstable, and poor Mary had to deal with me and my nonsense when I was at home. I had convinced her to do stuff with me a few times, and she would say yes to appease me sometimes, but she loved our baby so much that she made sure he came first. I was very toxic and evil and so selfish; I cared more about myself than her or our baby boy. But somehow God brought us through that rough and scary time, and a few months later, Mary became pregnant once again, and I really hoped I could straighten up.

Our son was just crawling and being a happy little boy when we found out Mary was pregnant with our second child. I was still working and supporting us, and I loved our little son, but I was struggling hard with my drug addiction. I had come close to losing my job a few times, but the oil field was booming, and I was not short of finding work if need be. I would quit using for as long as I could, and then I would get high again and mess everything up. Mary was definitely getting tired of my idiocy, but I was working, so she didn't say anything.

Soon enough, she started showing the famous baby bump, and I knew things were going to have to change. I had tried to stop doing drugs and looking at pornography, but it was something that had become very difficult. I was prone to addiction, and it was gonna take everything I had to stop. These doors I had opened were not easily closed. I loved Mary, and even though we were not married, I definitely wanted to be married to her. If I could have just straightened up long enough to buy her a ring and actually do it, I would have been a better man for it. Mary was a beautiful woman, and I was lucky to have her…I really was. And here she was pregnant with my fourth child, and I was so determined to straighten up.

Jocelyn and Noah had come to visit me and finally met Jonah and had a really fun time getting to know him. Mary was a very good mother as was Sofia, and I am thankful till this very day that God blessed me with these two women in my life. Mary was not working anymore since giving birth to our son, and it was up to me to work and support us. I would be sober for a little while until somebody from work would give me drugs, and I would be high for a day or two. And then I would quit for as long as I could and once again try to manage a normal life with Mary. I took her for granted, and I figured I could pretty much do drugs when I wanted too as long as I didn't cheat. And that was something I had given up since we first moved into together, and I was trying my best to be faithful. I really didn't have the time or energy to cheat on her because I was always working. And she was pregnant with our second child, so it was time to give her some respect and do my best for our lives.

I lost my job with my father because of my drug addiction and finally started to burn myself out. It was not easy like it was before, and all of it really started to catch up with me. I ended up getting in trouble with the law again for the same stuff I was in trouble with before. Writing bad checks back when I was still with Sofia, they charged me with one more check they had found. That check was for a really small amount, and I had to go serve three months in a halfway house but no prison or jail.

Mary and I moved to a nicer place in a better neighborhood while I was going through all my legal troubles, and that made things a little easier. I was working on the oil rigs again and providing for us while I served my sentence. I had finally quit doing drugs for a while and gave Mary and Jonah a little bit of peace. Around this same time, she finally gave birth to a beautiful little baby girl, and we named her Helena after my grandmother Helen. She was tan-skinned and very beautiful... I was so happy to have another daughter. Mary would bring them to see me, and we would spend time together. Mary was turning into a responsible mother and took good care of our children. She was faithful at this time and that really made me happy because I knew she was mine. I loved her very much, and I quit doing drugs and was hopeful that our lives would change for the better. But again, we did not go to church or pray to God, and I was still running from him, and I wanted to make something out of myself. I had big dreams of becoming a rapper, and I used this time to work out and practice my craft. I was very ambitious and in tune with the music of the moment, and I just knew I was gonna be big one day. I was released from my sentence and immediately came home and started writing music. I was staying sober, and I was young and decent looking, and I had a good-looking woman and beautiful children. I had it all. Any man would be envious of what God had given me. And there were a lot of guys after my girlfriend, and I knew that, but I knew she was mine, so it didn't affect me much.

My older children had moved back to Colorado, and I was so excited to see them again, and believe me, it was a joyous time. Jocelyn was seven years old now, and Noah was five. They were gone for a whole two years. Jonah was one years old, and Helena was just a little baby, and my life was complete. I was recording music and trying to make something out of my broken life and leaving my past behind me. Mary was a full-time mom, and I tried my best to give her everything I possibly could. My family was depending on me, and I was not gonna let them down anymore because they deserved the very best. I was twenty-seven years old now and was ready to be fully committed to Mary, and I wanted to marry her. I bought her a new vehicle and was working nonstop to give us a better life. But satan was creeping and making plans to destroy us and our little family, but I was sober for now, and I wanted it to stay that way.

CHAPTER 6

Lost in Sin

I had my family back together again, and I spent as much time as I could with my children and Mary. I loved this woman, and I wanted to make her happy as much as possible, and it wasn't easy. She was very beautiful, and I was very possessive and protective over her and for good reason. She was faithful for the most part, but she had her shortcomings, and she had cheated in the past. And I never really forgave her or trusted her like I should have, so that left an open invitation for the enemy to come in.

I was trying my best to stay sober, but I kept running into people who sold drugs, and I would keep their numbers "just in case." But that "just in case" was also an open invite for the enemy to come through and destroy our lives. And believe me, it wasn't long before I had called them and started getting high again, and that was a very sad time. I could remember the look on Mary's face the first time she came home with our children and caught me doing drugs in the house again. It was a look of disappointment, hurt, and anger, but I didn't care because at that moment, I only cared about myself. I had stayed sober for a really long time, and during that time, all I thought about was doing drugs. And when I finally did, I had let so many people down, and that was a very sad moment in my life. I would be high for a night or two, and then I would come down and sober up, and we would brush it under the rug and act like everything was ok. I would ask her to forgive me, and she would, and we would be together and act like nothing had ever happened. But it would happen again a month later and then two weeks after that and another month after that. There was no rhyme or reason for this. If I was happy, I would get high. If I was sad, I would get high. If I was mad, it would definitely occur. It was an endless cycle of drug abuse and abuse toward my small helpless family whom I thought I loved.

It was easy to hide it from my young children because I would come home with the drugs and lock myself in the room and get high. Mary would sleep with the kids in their room and not disturb me. And that was so abusive and ungodly to do that to my innocent little family, but I didn't care because the desire to get high was so strong that nothing or nobody could stop me. Mary would do this as a survival mechanism of protecting our children from me when I wasn't in my right mind. And protecting herself by not fighting with me or causing any kind of disruption in our small household because I was working, and she wasn't. She and the children were fully dependent on me, and she was just trying to survive. At that moment, she didn't have a voice because she was too scared to say anything, and I would always regret that. But she also knew it was only gonna last for a day or two, and things would go back to normal. If this life we had at this moment was anything, any person in their right mind would consider normal. I hated myself, and I hated my life and everything I had become and hadn't become. And satan would put hateful evil thoughts in my head before I would use, and I would always get the same depressing feeling. I just felt the hopelessness and despair of this life I had created with a woman who I didn't trust and who didn't trust me. And I would lock myself in the room away from my children and Mary and ignore them for days while I got high. I had a computer in the room, and I would look at pornography and think lustful thoughts while smoking drugs and hurting my little family. And this cycle continued because I was backsliding, and Mary was not saved, and God was not invited into our household or our lives. And we carried on like this for a long time, and she would love me less and less every single time.

My older kids would come and visit, and I was always able to maintain myself around them, and they never knew what I did. And the smaller ones never knew because Mary and I hid it from them. And I would sometimes pressure her into doing stuff with me, and she would give in now and then out of her own desires or just to make me happy. I was a selfish man, and I didn't deserve this woman or this family that God had given me. I was supposed to be their protector and provider, and even though I had provided for them, I was not protecting them. And again, people wondered how this woman could stay with someone like myself and how dumb could she possibly be. But you gotta understand I was young, decent-looking, and very charismatic when I was sober. And I was sober about 90 percent of the time, but it was just those days where no one saw me but her and my children that I would get away with this. It would happen on a Friday and end on a Sunday, and Monday, I would be back to work. I was a hard worker, and that was the only security I provided for her and my kids. This behavior went on for years, and I don't know how we stayed together or raised our children through all this, but we did. Mary was a good mother and put our children first, and I always appreciated that. I loved my children too, but this bad habit I had was something I also loved. Even though I kept doing it, I would always promise her that this would be the last time, and she would believe me. But it was never the last time, and she would eventually stop believing me and believing in me. She lost respect for me and soon just became numb to my madness. I hated myself for letting her become so distant and cold, but this discouraging reality would fuel my addiction even more.

Mary's distance left me feeling alone, and I started gaining a presence on social media with my fledgling rap career, which opened up the possibilities of talking to other women, and I would get by with that. I needed constant affirmation, and I would get that on social media because I had ruined my relationship with Mary. We needed serious help, and she had become very indifferent toward me and used me for what she needed, and that was support for her and our children. I loved her, and I knew I had screwed things up permanently, but deep down, I guess I felt we still had a chance.

Talking to other women on social media became a new addiction, and I knew it was wrong, but I had an unfaithful heart. Mary had been unfaithful too, but she was smarter than I was, and she knew to stay home and take care of our children first. But there were times when she would get dressed up and go out with her sister and do things with other people. She would come home at two or three in the morning, and it would be a big fight. Her sister did not have any respect for me and was a constant thorn in my and Mary's relationship.

Mary was beautiful, and she was damaged from past relationships and from the things I had done to her. I was abusive toward her emotionally, and a couple times, it had gotten physical. She was very small and petite, and looking back in time, I regret all the abuse I put her through, especially in dealing with me. The worst abuse was me locked in the room, doing drugs and abandoning my family for days on end. That drug was so very addicting and so horrible to my body physically and my mind mentally. It would take me to another world, where I didn't care about anything or anyone, and I would hurt my children emotionally. Even though they didn't know what was going on, it was still a horrible abuse toward them. I hated myself…I would get high on this drug and think bad evil thoughts toward Mary, who was asleep with my children in the next room, trying to cope with my insanity. She deserved so much better and so did my children. Regardless of her shortcomings, no woman deserves this type of abuse in any relationship.

Every time I would get high, I would get progressively worse. At first, I was just into watching pornography, and then I would always sleep with Mary when I was coming down. But then Mary started saying no and not letting me sleep with her; I would get upset and storm out. I started going out and driving around, looking for somewhere else to go. I started to want to find someone who would hang out with me when I was high. I would meet different women off social media, and they would see me high and want nothing more to do with me. Nobody wanted anything to do with me when I was on drugs, and that used to frustrate me even more. But I was talking to women behind Mary's back and disrespecting her and my children by acting single. I figured since Mary had cheated on me before that I was in the right to cheat back, which was very wrong.

When I was sober, I loved Mary and looked past all her flaws, and she would look past all of mine. But when I would get high on this horrible drug, it would unlock all my ungodly desires, and I would want to be unfaithful. It started with pornography and ended with me physically going out and looking for other women. I was handsome and charismatic when I was sober and had no problem with the opposite gender. But when I was high, I was a mess, and women could spot a sinking ship from a mile away. I would sober up for a while for as long as I could, and then like clockwork, I would go on a bender for two or three days now. But when it was all over, I would spend time with my kids and try to act like nothing had happened. I expected Mary to do the same, and she would…she would forgive me every time because I was a good father sober. I kept trying to fight the urge to do these evil things and would stay sober for a couple months…just long enough to reconcile my relationship with Mary.

I tried my best to treat her right and be faithful even though I was still talking to other women on social media and acting single. I was trying to stay clean, and all I wanted was Mary to be my wife and for us to have a good relationship. We would start to get close again, and we would take our kids to the park and to the movies. I loved my children, and I always did my best to give them what they needed and provide for them. I would do everything I could for Mary and give her everything she wanted or needed. She was a simple woman who only wanted to be taken care of and wanted security for our family. She wanted a stable relationship and home life for our children, and those were things that the enemy didn't want me to provide for them, but I was trying my best to make that happen.

I asked Mary to marry me one evening, and with much hesitation, she finally said yes, and I was very happy. I bought her a ring and we went down to the courthouse and tied the knot in shotgun fashion. I was feeling the conviction of God, and I kept trying to run away, and I figured getting married would appease him. He was on my mind a lot because I knew the promises I had made to him when

I was young, but I was now thirty-two, and the years were flying by with Mary. He never forgot the promise I told him when I was fifteen, and that was that I would come back when I was thirty. I had been feeling so much guilt about everything we had gone through, and I thought getting married would help ease it. I remember the day we tied the knot, Mary started crying…tears of sadness, not joy, and that bothered me very much. She would never take my last name, and that was something that hurt me a lot. I knew the things I had done to her were horrible, and that I needed to come clean, but that was not gonna happen. Instead we were doing okay for a couple months, and then like clockwork, satan would come to kill, steal, and destroy once again. I had lost some really good jobs because of my drug addiction, and that was a problem for Mary. She didn't want me to lose work because it meant unsteadiness and more worries for her. But I had been at the same job for a while, and we were doing well until I met someone else at work who sold that drug, and for me, the urge was too much for me to say no to.

I was a married man now, and I had a lot of responsibilities in my life, and I had no room for error, but that wouldn't stop my addiction. I started getting dope from a new dealer who I worked with, and my life started to crumble once again. I would get so high that I couldn't go to work, and I would get in trouble and eventually fired. This was a pattern that was starting to become a really big problem, and I would have to find another job. I would get so high that I couldn't go out in public because I would stutter and look like a mess. My movements were jerky, and my heart would be pounding, and my veins enlarged. I was embarrassed of myself, and I would hide at home, locked in a room. Mary was tired of it, and she started to rebel against this insanity and fight for her and our children. She would lock me out of the house and refuse to let me in, and this would make me angry. It was a constant fight, and my addiction was getting worse and worse by the day. The things I would do on this drug were getting stupider, and my thought process was not very good at all. I would accuse Mary of being unfaithful and search through her personal belongings and her phone. Calling numbers and upsetting family members that were her personal contacts. I had even ended up in jail again because of some huge fights while I was high, and this was truly disturbing. I was a ticking time bomb and an embarrassment to her and our children, and people were starting to notice.

Mary started to realize I was being unfaithful behind her back and decided to do the same. Our relationship should have been over right then and there, but somehow we went on. I didn't want her to leave me physically, but she had already left me emotionally. Our children were older now and were starting to see us argue and go at it physically, and they knew something wasn't right with their dad. Mary had flat out told me that she didn't love me anymore, and that tore deep into my soul. So in my eyes, our relationship was over, and all I was doing was supporting her, and I meant nothing to her. I would leave the house to go get high, and I would be gone for days at a time. I would get so high that I didn't know where I was at anymore, and I would blackout. I would rent hotel rooms and lock myself in the room for days and days on end. I would call different women over to come see me, and they would get so scared and leave in fear. I remember my kids seeing me like this, and they started crying because I was so high and not in my right state of mind. I felt so bad, and it hurt because I remember seeing my father just like this when I was thirteen. The cycle had come full circle, and now I was doing the same things to my children. I just wanted to forget the reality of this life that I had ruined, but in reality, I was ruining five other lives.

My oldest daughter was twelve now, and my son Noah was ten, and I was missing their basketball and baseball games because I was either high or in jail. My younger children were figuring out that something wasn't right with Dad and would hide every time I would come home messed up. I was being unfaithful to Mary in my thoughts and in my actions every chance I could. I let the enemy put bad thoughts about her in my head, and I didn't trust her anymore because she was cheating on me. I had found out about her talking to other men, and I just flipped out and was so angry. I wouldn't let her go to sleep until she admitted to me what she had done. She finally had told me that her sister had introduced her to someone, and she had seen him a couple of times. I was so mad and hurt, but what could I do? I was doing the same thing; I felt like such a hypocrite.

The urge to get high grew so bad that I would go out looking for it and put myself in so many compromising situations. I didn't care anymore, and I would do whatever I had to do to get it, and I didn't care about my family at home. I started to meet party girls who like to get high too, and so I didn't scare them. They would do whatever I asked as long as I was getting them messed up and paying for it. My family was at home, and they were the last thing on my mind because I just wanted to have a good time. These women had poor morals, and I was careful not to sleep with them out of fear of giving something to my wife at home. But other than that, I just enjoyed their company because for years, I had done this drug alone. It was a lonely road that I had made for myself, and my young spouse was home alone with the kids, hurt and indifferent toward me. We would get into huge fights in front of our children every time I would come home, and our kids were always afraid. I had lost my marriage to my addiction, and the only thing I was to her now was a paycheck. She was working now and having to help pay bills, and she wasn't too fond of that. It wasn't a fifty-fifty relationship. Most of the responsibility was left on my shoulders, and I was failing miserably. I was a lost cause, and Mary no longer saw hope in me, and I no longer saw any hope in myself either. I hated myself so much. Deep down, I wanted to end my life, but I didn't want to hurt my children any more than I already had.

Even when I was completely sober, I still looked a mess, and any smart person could tell something wasn't right with me. My bosses and employers could tell something wasn't right, and the first time I would call in because I was under the influence, they would fire me. I lost a lot of good-paying stable jobs because of my drug addiction. I had brought bad and evil spirits into our home without realizing it. Looking at pornography and doing drugs in the room had invited some dark spirits that had gone unnoticed. Until one day, I was fighting with Mary over my phone and had accidentally snapped a picture in our bedroom. Later on, I looked at the pic and saw a small face looking at Mary from under the covers, and none of our kids were home. I was so scared I called my mother who came over and prayed for our place. I knew I had screwed up.

When I would do drugs, I could feel something very dark around me, and no one wanted anything to do with that. Satan had such a strong grip on my life, and he wanted my soul. These bad suicidal thoughts were getting worse and worse every time, and I knew they were coming from him. Mary would come home and find me high and immediately leave with the kids and not return. I would not even care because I wanted to be high and not be around her or my children. I was a horrible person, and there was no turning back from this point on. I didn't want to even try anymore, and I felt I had no one to turn to. I had no friends and no positive influences in my life, except my parents. But I hid my addiction from them because I would be embarrassed if they found out what their only son had turned into. I was a monster with an addiction as big as the moon, and it weighed on me so heavy. I felt there was no longer any hope in this life, and I had done too many bad things in my life to turn back.

My wife didn't love me any longer, and that hurt me very much, but that didn't stop me. I knew that I had done this to myself, but the thought of losing her, I could not even bear. She no longer wanted to be with me, and she found me repulsive and embarrassing. I had done so many stupid things being high and not in my right mind that she finally had enough. The enemy used her indifference toward me to try to ruin our relationship and end our marriage for good. I felt so worthless and I was lost and my heavy heart was broken.

Mary was such a beautiful woman, but that's all I had ever seen was her beauty. I never paid attention to her heart. All the years with her, I never really had gotten to know her or who she really was. I was lost to this world, and I had lost all my hopes and dreams, and my reality became a real nightmare. I had lost my mind in this world of hurt and pain and addiction, and I had lost my wife's love and affection. I had nowhere to go…I finally had realized I was lost in drugs. I was lost in infidelities, I was lost in pornography, I was lost in sin.

CHAPTER 7

The Running Man

I was losing my relationship with Mary very fast, and all my sins and shortcomings were starting to work against me. I was no longer a good father, and my children were suffering because of my poor decisions. My drug addiction was in full effect, and my infidelities had been brought to light on more than a few occasions. Mary knew I was a cheater, and I was not doing my part as a husband in providing financial security and wellness. I was battling this addiction on my own, but my family was the one being put through it all. I would get caught for everything. I was very sloppy, and I didn't even try to hide things from her anymore. What was the point? She had told me over and over again that she was no longer in love with me. I was just barely hanging on by a thread, and I was in utter turmoil inside and out. We had been in some huge fights, and she was so fed up with me she would scream at the top of her lungs so the neighbors could hear and most certainly call the cops, and they would show up and arrest me. She definitely didn't care what happened to me anymore, and she showed that more and more every day.

I was thirty-five years old now, and she was thirty-three, and we had been together for over ten years. I was working on a second rap album, and I had high hopes for success this time. But this drug addiction kept taking those hopes away from me, and I felt like a helpless prisoner of my own doing. I was still running from a loving, caring God who only had my best interest at heart.

When I look back at this time, it was ridiculous and moronic that I just didn't get on my knees and give my life back to him. I was still chasing this big dream of becoming a famous rap star, and I just knew in my heart that I could do it. I thought if I did that Mary would ultimately forgive me and love me again, but that dream was redundant and far-fetched. I could barely stay sober long enough to complete the recording of the album, and I finally did do that. The album was innovative and cool and not that bad for an amateur recording artist. But these dreams and aspirations just brought more turmoil to my already unhealthy toxic relationship. I had no peace and no support system with Mary, and it was very hard to accomplish anything besides bringing home a paycheck. She was busy raising our children, and I was busy being a selfish fool, chasing pipe dreams… with no pun intended.

I had put this album out for sale, and it was gonna be a long road to success, and I just didn't have the finances or energy anymore to keep going with it. The album had cost a lot of money to make, and I was determined to at least make that back, and I did do that. My family went without for so long while I was recording the album, and I had the highest hopes that it would be successful. But when I listened to the music and heard what I was ultimately saying, I felt the conviction of God, and I knew it wasn't right. I knew in my heart that I couldn't go any further with it, and God was not gonna let it happen. Because even though I wasn't serving him, he was not gonna let me become this famous rap star that I so desperately needed to become. I knew I was leading people down the wrong path with my careless words; these lyrics in my songs were not very humble or positive. I made the money back that I had initially invested in it, and I quit. Needless to say, Mary looked at me like a failure, and that just fueled my addiction even more. I was a huge failure in life, and I watched all my dreams go up in smoke as I smoked them away with this horrible drug.

That drug came from Mexico and was big business for the cartels who would ship it in by the pounds. I had watched it tear families apart and had read about the murders and horrors that go along with it. That drug was invented by chemists back in the early 1900s and was used to keep nazi soldiers awake in war. It was called speed back then, and now it went by its more familiar name of methamphetamine. It was an evil narcotic that had no place in society, but yet it was a huge problem in many countries, including America. This drug came straight from the pits of hell and had ruined so many people's lives and torn families apart, including mine. It was so highly addictive and pleasurable that it would make people not care about anything, including their personal relationships and families. I had done this drug so much that I was no longer trusted by my significant other, and she felt she was no longer in love. There was no point in staying sober anymore because my reality was so horrible to myself and everyone around me. But the reality I had created for my children was far worse, and that fact tore my heart to pieces. I loved my children, and my oldest was fifteen by now and becoming a young woman. I was not there for her like I should have been, and I will always regret that in hindsight when I look back at my sinful life. Her brother Noah, my oldest son, was thirteen, and he needed a steady, stable father, and I could not give that to him, and it hurts still to this day.

My two younger children with Mary were nine and seven at the time, Jonah being the oldest and Helena being the youngest, and they had seen so much at this point in their lives. They needed a daddy who loved them more than he loved himself. But instead they had a dad who loved getting high more than he loved anything else, and he needed to repent to God. I was looked at as a liar and a cheat, and I had no moral compass when it came to my addiction. I was a sinking ship in an ocean of lies and deceit, and nobody could trust me anymore, and I couldn't even trust myself.

The enemy wanted to destroy my family, and what he really wanted was my children and their bright future. He knew Mary's weaknesses, and he definitely knew mine, and he would use those things against us. He wanted me dead or in jail, and my behavior definitely put those options in the realm of possibilities. And then Mary and my children would be open season to destroy their lives through mine. We were struggling from check to check, and I was always having to find another job after a three-day bender because I would show up to work late and act like nothing had happened. But for some reason, we held on, and Mary kept working and taking care of our children while I continued to put her through hell. I could barely function, and my problems were getting bigger, and they were not going away anytime soon. I didn't know what to do anymore; I was lost in my sin and confused on who to turn too. All my so-called friends I had made in the past few years were drug dealers and drug users and people who had no moral compass either. The benders were getting worse and worse, and I started doing some really stupid things while I was high.

One cold winter night, I came home and was playing with my children while Mary was taking a shower. She always took her phone with her, but this time, she had left it on the couch, and it started buzzing. I told my kids to hold on, and I got up to see who it was, and to my surprise, her phone was unlocked. She had a message, saying, "What's up, babe?" My head started pounding, and my heart raced. I messaged back immediately, pretending to be her, and asked who this was texting her. This person sent a picture of himself and said he wanted to meet up again, and I just flew into a rage. I called him up and cussed him out and told him she was married and never to call her again. I waited for her to get out of the shower, and I was so mad, and she tried to deny it, but I was not having it. I didn't even stop to look at my kids who were still sitting on the floor, probably dumbfounded. I just grabbed all my stuff and left slamming the door. I knew I did this to myself and my relationship. I ruined it because of my addiction. But deep down, I truly loved this woman, and I couldn't deal with the reality of where our relationship was at this point. I couldn't get to the drug dealer's house fast enough, and I jumped out of the car and pounded on his door. I bought a lot of drugs from him that night, and I rented a hotel room with the very last of my money. I started getting high, and I couldn't stop, and I did it for what must have been days. I called over different women to come see me, and they would come over two at a time and would literally be so afraid at what they saw…they would just leave. I was a monster, and I opened doors that couldn't be closed.

After this horrific bender, I decided to go home and sneak in to try to retrieve some of my belongings. Mary took one look at me and started screaming at the top of her lungs. I freaked out because I was so high… I ran out of the apartment and ran across the street where the cops were waiting, and they arrested me. One cop was looking at me very suspiciously because it was cold outside, and I was sweating profusely. He put his hand on his gun like he was ready to shoot, and I definitely could see it in his expression. I had tossed the drugs I had on me while I was being patted down, and the rest, I dumped in the cop car on the way to jail. I was booked on a trespassing charge, and I sat in jail for three months.

Coming down off this high was horrible, and it took me a couple weeks to get back to normal.

A wonderful lady named sister Margo, who ran the jail ministry, kept sending inmates to tell me to come down and see her. I refused out of embarrassment, but she would send more inmates to come and tell me that she was praying for me and that God loved me.

While I was in there, another inmate who was there on a murder charge decided to pass me a Bible. I didn't want anything to do with it because it was a relic from my past, and I wanted nothing more to do with God. I hated it, I hated God, I hated this heaviness in my heart, and at this moment, I hated myself. That Bible sat on my bed for another two weeks, but I couldn't stop thinking about it. I knew I wasn't getting out anytime soon, so I said to myself, "It can't hurt to open it," and I sat in my jail cell and read that book.

From front to back, I read the whole Bible and read the stories of this mighty God who loved his people so much that he would do anything for them, including becoming a human to die for them so they could be forgiven. That story resonated with me so hard in that jail cell, and I began to cry, and I asked God to forgive me. I remembered the story my aunt had told me when I was just a little boy about this man who had made a great sacrifice for mankind. That he had died for me and all of humanity, and his name was Jesus Christ. I had forgotten this man and what he had done for me and my children and my lonely wife at home. I had been running from God for twenty years, and I couldn't run anymore, and I was done running. I had ruined my marriage to a woman who I truly loved, and I was a bad father to my four children that I also truly loved. I couldn't stop crying as my life flashed before my eyes, and I saw all the bad things I had done. It was such a horrible feeling knowing I did this to my family, and I was so ashamed. What had I become in this life? What had I done to this family that God had given to me? I abused it and misused it, and I was a drug addict now and a womanizer and just a complete douchebag. I needed God, and I needed him now more than ever as I sat in that jail cell. I prayed and prayed and asked for forgiveness every single day until they finally called my name to pack it up, and I was released.

It was hard getting out of jail and going back to a normal life after that surreal experience of crying out and asking God for forgiveness. Mary started crying when I walked through the door, and she just hugged me for a really long time. I loved this woman, and my absence I believe made her realize that she loved me. I realized I needed God, and that I couldn't go back to my old ways because of my experience in jail. So Mary and I tried again, and we started to go to church and go to a Sunday night Bible study. I was struggling with work and living check to check, and things were still really hard between us. She started to trust me again, but we still had a lot of issues to work out because we both had hurt each other very badly, but my addiction had really devastated us. It wasn't gonna be that easy to quit because I still had all the same drug dealer friends constantly texting me, telling me to come by, and my sobriety was short-lived. It wasn't too long before I started getting high again, and Mary was so angry and hurt. But this time, it was far worse, and my addiction had grown bigger. I had finally surrendered to God, but because I didn't take it seriously when I got out, it was open season with the enemy. I was right back to it after a few short months of sobriety, and it was like I never stopped. Mary would just lock herself in the room and not let me in, and I would go out and just drive around high. I wouldn't come home for days and weeks now while I was on these huge horrible benders. I didn't want to sober up or come down from my high because I had backslidden, and I felt no hope again. My experience in jail with God was short-lived, and I went on like it had never happened, but it did. God didn't forget what had happened in that jail cell, and he was not gonna let me go back to my sinful life that easily.

I still had a case over my head, and I had to go back to jail, but I was allowed to go to work and support my family. It was the best thing that could have happened to me because I couldn't get high, and I had to maintain steady employment. I did very well in this program, and I tried my best, and I was sober for a long time. Mary was going to church still and had given her life to God, and she was taking my children every Sunday. I appreciated that because I knew she was a good mother with a good heart, and she did a great job raising our children. I was tired of being broke and not supporting my family in the right way. We had been together for many years and still living in a two-bedroom apartment, and my kids needed their own rooms. I was frustrated with my life and still working these low-paying dead-end jobs.

One day, I was overcome by the Holy Spirit, and I fell to my knees, crying.

I said, "God, please forgive me…please…please forgive me! I'm tired of running away from you, and I'm tired of this sinful lustful life I have lived! I don't know how to serve you anymore, but please come back in my life and help me change it. Give me peace, Lord!" And I felt the loving warmth of the Holy Spirit, and I knew at that moment, things were about to change for the better.

Immediately the very next day, I was hired for a well-paying job, delivering roof shingles. I worked hard and was shown favor from all the bosses, and within six months, I had attained my CDL and was running my own crew. The paychecks were great, and I appreciated my job, and I knew in my heart that God had given me this opportunity. I was supporting my family and staying sober and was back home where I belonged.

Mary and I were trying to reconcile again, and man, I truly loved this woman, and it was awesome to see her through sober eyes. I knew in my heart that God had given me this woman to love and support, and I thanked him for that. I knew I struggled so hard with my addiction, but right now, I stood a fighting chance. And we had a chance to fix our marriage and love each other in the right way and be good parents to our children as they were growing up and becoming teens. I watched my credit score shoot up to seven hundred, which was unimaginable to me a year before. I bought a new vehicle and started paying off all our bills and working on finding a home. I was making huge money, and I was so thankful to God because I knew it was all because of him, and I started to feel invincible. I had made it through this nightmare unscathed, and I still had my beautiful wife and amazing children. We moved into a really nice four-bedroom home and had all new furniture and new everything. My kids were so happy, and Mary was happy, and I knew I did it all with the help of God. I finally gave my family the peace and comfort that they yearned for and that they deserved. My oldest son and daughter had rooms there, and my youngest both had their own rooms also. It was a great feeling, and Mary and I were working together to support our children, and everything was great. I was sober, and I was working hard, and God had changed my whole life in the matter of one year after I had fully surrendered to him. It was an amazing powerful testimony of an amazing powerful God. Mary and I were going to church and to a Sunday night Bible study.

Bible study was awesome, and I was still pretty rough around the edges, but the people there were devout older Christians and great mentors for Mary and me. We had some pretty awesome testimonies of what God had brought us through, but we were still not fully living for him. We were trying though, and we definitely had a budding faith that was growing inside us.

One Sunday evening, after our group had prayed, Brother Steve had a prophetic word from God for Mary and me. Brother Steve was a pastor, and he was a very godly man that I had really looked up to. He led the Bible study and led us in prayer that evening.

He looked right at me and said, "God told me to tell you that you are going to be a pastor for the Lord." And then he turned to Mary and told her, "'Are you ready to become a pastor's wife?'"

And that prophetic word shook me to my core because I knew it was from God, and that it was 100 percent true. I had been prophesied to as a kid two separate times and basically told almost the exact same thing by two other pastors. And now I'm being told this once again at thirty-seven years old? But I just took it with a grain of salt because it was just too hard for me to fathom. I don't know what Mary was thinking; I'm sure it was hard for her to believe too. She knew about what had been told to me as a young kid, but now she had witnessed it firsthand. I was far from a godly pastor. I was a horrible person but one who definitely believed that there was a God. And now the third time hearing it, I knew it was real, and God had bigger plans for me. But the enemy also had a plan to destroy me and never let God's plan see light of day. I was holding my family up with my wife's help, and I needed her full support. But the enemy was gonna use people to draw her away and cause her to be unsupportive.

Around this same time, one of her sisters started inviting her to some strange business group. Men and women (all Hispanic) would gather at a hotel for a whole weekend and hangout and motivate each other…to do what? I had no idea. It was very suspicious, I didn't care for it all, and I did not approve of what she was doing. She started missing Bible studies and became more and more distant.

One evening, she called while I was in Bible study and told me she was gonna start giving this business group money. I was upset, but I couldn't tell her what to do because I felt guilty for everything I had done, so I just let it go. And she was gone all weekend, leaving me with the kids, and we didn't know what to think of it. Around this same time, I decided it was time to get baptized, and Mary and I brought all the kids to church to witness this.

Pastor Rigo let me speak a few words before he immersed me in the lukewarm water. I told my kids that I loved them, and I was doing it for them, and that I wanted to change my life. But I should have been doing it for myself and my personal relationship with Christ. Later that night, Mary and I were asleep, and I could feel something staring at me, and it was very angry. I tried to open my eyes, and when I did, I saw a nine-foot tall black shadow standing over me, breathing heavy and in anger. I was so scared that I couldn't move, and I was trying to rebuke him in the name of Jesus Christ. Mary woke up and tried to wake me, and when I awoke, it disappeared into the wall. I was wrestling with something much bigger than me, but it wasn't bigger than Jesus. What I saw was a demon from hell angry at me for giving my life to God.

One evening, some random guy showed up at my home and knocked on my door and asked me if I got high. I told him I was clean, and that he needed to leave, but before he did, he handed me a bag of drugs. I don't know who he was or how he knew what I did, but it didn't take long before I was locked in the bathroom. And the kids were asleep, and Mary was gone, and so I got away with it. And this guy kept coming and selling it to me on the weekends when Mary was with her group. I stopped going to church and Bible study, and my life slowly started to fall apart again. I started seeing pictures of my wife on Facebook all dressed up with these people from this strange group. I started becoming really resentful of her, and I started talking to other women online.

Mary came home and caught me high again, and she just closed herself off to me completely. We were once again headed for destruction, and the enemy had a hold on me so strong that there was no coming back from this. My addiction was back and with a vengeance, and Mary was off doing God knows what with God knows who. Our marriage was falling apart at the seams, and I was falling apart also. I started missing work because I was too high to function, and my job was on the line. I was back to where I started, but now my addiction was one hundred times worse.

CHAPTER 8

A Sinking Ship

My marriage was falling apart right before my eyes, and I didn't even care anymore because I was upset with Mary. I found moving boxes in the garage that she was bringing home from work, so I knew she was planning on leaving me. Satan had a grip on our lives more than ever now because we had been making an effort to go to church again, and then we stopped. I was working hard to give this woman everything I possibly could, and she was working hard to give this business group everything. I was hurt and angry with her, and so I started talking to other women online. My old unfaithful habit was back and at full steam, and my heart was full of resentment and anger. I was talking to every woman who would give me a chance, and I started to go out and meet up with them. I made a huge effort to stay sober so I wouldn't scare them off as per usual. I just wanted to have fun with them and have a nice conversation and feel wanted and admired. With these other women, I could be anybody I wanted to be, and I didn't have to be who I really was. My low self-esteem was in full effect, and I needed an attractive woman sitting in front of me to feel better about myself. But it was all lies, and I was a liar and a cheater, and I felt I no longer loved Mary. Her life was a secret, and she was doing what she pleased, and I felt I just was a paycheck to her. And that hurt me to think about, but I kept supporting my family because that was my job, and I loved my children.

One Friday evening, I decided to go out and meet up with a couple women who I had been talking to online. We met at a bar and had some drinks together, and we had a good time while Mary was at home taking care of our children. These women saw that I took care of myself and had money and they were having me buy all their cocktails. They were taking turns dancing with me and telling me how handsome I was. I was eating it up like you wouldn't believe, and these young party girls were just using me to get free drinks. It was the night before my son's thirteenth birthday, and I totally had forgotten about it. I wasn't talking to Mary anymore, and she wasn't talking to me either. I was out with these young females that night, buying them piña coladas and letting them use me. I was already hammered when they decided they wanted to go to a restaurant and eat. So we left in a hurry, and I could barely drive my car, swerving through traffic drunk just to get some food. These wild party girls ordered the most expensive items on the menu, and when the bill came, they all looked at me to pay for it. I wasn't having it, and so I decided I was gonna go get some drugs and get high instead. I told them I was gonna go use the restroom, and I booked it out the back door, jumped in my car, and left. I could barely drive as I headed to the dealer's house to go get some drugs. I was speeding and swerving, mad and hurt, and falling apart all at the same time. When all of a sudden, I looked in my rearview mirror to see cop lights flashing behind me, and my heart immediately sank. I pulled over to the side of the road, and the officers pulled me out at gunpoint and had me do a roadside sobriety test. I could barely stand let alone walk, and I was immediately placed in handcuffs and put in the back of the cop car. My car was towed away, and I was taken down to the police station and was booked on drunk driving charges. I had to call Mary to come pick me up, and she wasn't too happy, but of course, she did. It was a long drive home, and I was sick to my stomach, and I kept needing her to pull over so I could throw up.

The next day was my son's thirteenth birthday, and even though I was hung over and had gotten a DUI, I was so happy that I never made it to the drug dealer's house. If I would have made it, I would have been high, and I would have missed my son's birthday party. I drove a truck for a living with my CDL, and I had just gotten a bread delivery route that paid really well. What was I gonna tell my boss? I knew I was gonna lose my job and lose everything that I worked for, but I kept driving and kept making a paycheck. I couldn't afford to be honest and tell the truth. So I kept going and working like nothing had happened even though my license was now suspended, and I was in really big trouble.

I was still talking to different women online and decided to go out to dinner with one in particular that I really liked. She really liked me, and she was from a different city, so I figured it would be safe to go see her. I didn't tell her I was married, and she assumed I was single. Of course, she was very sweet, and we had a nice time. I was ready to start over and leave Mary because I felt hopeless in our broken relationship. I thought she was never going to love me like I wanted to be loved, and she was never gonna forgive me for everything I had done to her. So I was going to replace her and change my life…at least that was my idiotic thought at the time. I was really running from God and his calling that I knew for certain he had placed in my life. But God was about to take everything he had given me away from me. I had turned away from him when he wanted me the most, and I rejected his call once again. Satan wanted me out of the picture so he could rip my family apart piece by piece. And my glasshouse was about to come crashing down around me, and Mary had her bags packed.

One evening, I tried to go see this woman whom I was talking to, and I sent her a text, saying hi and asking how she was. She immediately texted me back and said she wanted nothing more to do with me because I was married. She somehow knew Mary's sister's sister-in-law, and it had all gotten back to Mary. I was dumbfounded and pissed off, and I drove home in a fury because I knew I was gonna be in trouble. I came through the front door, and Mary confronted me about everything she had heard, and I admitted to all of it as our children sat there listening. The whole house was sad, and Mary just locked herself in the room, and my kids went off to bed. I ended up at the drug dealer's house that night, bought drugs, and started getting high once again. I was so selfish and wanted people to feel sorry for me, but no one did, and I was slowly feeling my life being ripped away from me.

I bought more drugs than I had ever bought in my whole life, and I got so high that I didn't want to come down. And I didn't want to go home either because Mary and the kids were there, and they didn't need to see this. I was still going to work and driving my truck even after I had been up for days, and I was putting a lot of people in danger. I finally decided to go back home and sleep it off, and needless to say, it was not a very pleasant experience. Mary was totally cold to me and had her own agenda on what she was planning to do. I had a chance to go to sleep and not have any problems with Mary, but she was sleeping in another room, and that made me very upset. I had no leg to stand on whatsoever but I still decided to go fight with Mary and yell at her for not sleeping with me. And the fight broke out instantly, and we were screaming at each other from the top of our lungs. Our kids woke up and immediately started crying because of us yelling and seeing us starting to get physical. My older kids were not staying there anymore because of my drug use. And the younger ones had no choice but to deal with my drug addiction head on and witness their mother and me fighting. She started breaking everything, including the TV, and I knew I was gonna end up in jail if I didn't do something quick. She was hitting me and kicking me and screaming for the police, so I started to panic. I called my parents, which I rarely did, but I felt like it was an emergency and one I had definitely caused myself.

Within ten minutes, they showed up and told the kids to go to bed and told Mary to get her stuff and leave, which she did. I went to bed and woke up the next morning and went to work the next day like nothing had happened. But when I came home, my kids and Mary were gone and so was all their belongings. I was upset, and I felt really bad. I tried to call them, but no one would answer, so I went to my room, locked the door, and started to get high again. I kept getting high for the next couple of days and weeks, and I had no idea where Mary and my kids were. I tried calling and calling with no answer, so I kept using drugs and watching pornography. I went to work one day, and my boss found out that I had gotten a DUI and fired me on the spot.

He said, "I don't know what's wrong with you, but you really took a turn for the worse. May God help you."

And that was that, and that was my only income. It was gone, and I was about to go off the deep end. I went back home and kept getting high, and I knew I was gonna lose everything, but I didn't care anymore.

My younger kids had finally called me one day and said they wanted to come home, and that they missed the house. I asked them where they were at, and they told me that they were at a relative's home, but they didn't know the address. I told them to get me the address, and I would go get them, but I knew needed to sober up before I did.

The next day, they showed up without telling me, and I was still out of my mind, and they saw that and started crying. It was a sad, pathetic day in my life of sin, and it reminded me of when I had seen my father high when I was that exact same age. They called my oldest daughter to come pick them up; she had moved out months earlier. She showed up and started crying and yelling at me, and my heart just broke, but all I could do was yell back as I went and hid inside. I was a mess, and none of my kids should have seen me like that, but they did, and that was something they would never be able to erase from their mind. But everybody had left, and I was completely on my own now and with no income and a house to pay for. I stayed there for another two months, and I had different people over, trying to find a roommate. But when God gives you everything you had asked for and then you decide to disobey and spit in his face, he takes it all away. And I didn't stay in his word, and I wasn't praying everyday like I should have been. I should have been praying for my wife and my children, and of course, I never did. I was angry and hurt with Mary because she was angry and hurt with me. And she was gone, and she was never coming back, and it broke my heart, but I just couldn't stop doing drugs. It meant more to me obviously than my family had meant to me because I couldn't stop doing what I was doing. I had done this for years and years, and every time I relapsed, my addiction grew worse and worse. I sacrificed my whole family just to get high, and I let my salvation be taken away by the enemy.

I stayed for a couple more months after Mary and the kids left, and then I lost everything because I couldn't pay the rent. I moved out and moved back home with my parents and continued to struggle with my addiction, but I was trying my best to overcome it. My kids would come over and see me there, and they were just completely destroyed. At this same time, their mom had filed for divorce, and we were going to court on that matter. She was going on trips with her friends and enjoying her new life while I sat at home feeling like my heart had been ripped from my chest. It was hard for me, but I knew I did it all to myself, and I had tried to move on.

After a few months at home, I had found a townhome for rent and moved into it. I lived there for almost a year, but being on my own was difficult because I couldn't find any reason to stay sober. I tried dating other women, and they would treat me really well, but they were just a rebound for me. None of these women were Mary, and I knew that, and as soon I would get high on drugs, I would scare them away.

My oldest son Noah stayed with me and stuck by my side through the thick and thin, but after a while, he was fed up with me being on drugs. He would show up randomly and see me like that, and I knew that upset him, and I was a big disappointment to him. My younger children would come over unarranged, and it was the exact same thing. I was a complete loser and disappointment to every single one of my children. My oldest daughter Jocelyn was grown up now and living with her boyfriend, she wanted nothing more to do with me. I loved her very much and really regretted what had happened before when we all had lived together at that house. She watched her dad fall apart in front of her eyes and wanted nothing more to do with him. And how could I blame her? She was grown up now and beautiful and had her whole life ahead of her. My younger kids always gave me the benefit of the doubt, and they stuck by my side in hopes their dad would one day change. My life was a nightmare, and I was sorry that I had put my children through it all.

Mary had quickly filed for child support and spousal subsistence after our divorce was finalized. She had no more love for me and no remorse at all, and from here on out, it was gonna get really ugly. I struggled to pay my rent and pay my child support, and I finally had to move back home again. I worked hard and tried my best to stay sober at my parents' home, but it was still really difficult for me. My relapses were fewer and far between now, and I strived to stay sober and reconcile with my children. They forgave me, and they just wanted me to be a good father to them, and that's all I desired to be. I started going back to church and made my peace with God, and that was difficult at first. But I was really trying my best because it was expected of me, and really I had no other choice. But every couple of months, I would get really depressed and upset with myself and go out and get messed up on drugs. I would stay gone for a couple of days and then come home and go back to work. Drugs had no place in my life any longer, but I would still go out and try to find them, which I did, but God was now making things very difficult for me.

Every time I would relapse, the situations were getting far worse and more desperate, and I was always nervous and uneasy. The enemy didn't want to let me go until I was in jail or dead because he didn't want me to ever fulfill my calling. And I knew it, and it started to consume me, and I couldn't stop thinking about it. But the desire to get high was worse than ever, and I would go out and have to look for it, and I met some really sketchy people along the way. And every time I would be sitting in these dope houses, nervous, and waiting to buy drugs, the people around me were uneasy too. They could sense something that they didn't like and would tell me to leave. They would always say, "I don't know what it is, man…but you don't belong here," and they would kick me out. And I would drive around until I could acquire what I was looking for and finally get high. I would feel so guilty and ashamed of myself that it was unbearable, and I was just a complete mess.

One night, I had met a young man who sold dope, and I some-how convinced him to sell me some drugs. The transaction went smooth, and we exchanged numbers so I could keep buying from him. Later that night, he had his girlfriend call me and ask for a ride with the promise of more drugs. It was totally sketchy, and I knew I had to stop dealing with these types of people, but the desire for this drug was unbearable, and I quickly said okay. I drove over to their apartment in the projects and picked her up and asked where she needed to go. She hesitated, and I sensed something wasn't right, and I told her that she needed to get out of my vehicle.

All of a sudden, she yelled, "Get him!"

Her boyfriend and his buddies ran up on me from both sides. He looked around quickly and pulled a gun out of his waistband, cocked it, and pointed it at my head. All I could think about at that moment were my children.

He said, "Give me all your money!"

I looked to my right and told that woman to "get the hell out of my car!" I thought about my whole life at that very instant and how my kids would feel if I was shot and killed like this. I knew I could beat this guy up, but he had a gun pointing at my head and his buddies all had guns too. This woman wouldn't get out of my car, and this man who had sold drugs to me earlier was high out of his mind himself. I then thought about when I was five years old and how I gave my life to Christ and how much I loved him as a kid. I thought about my ex-wife and how much we used to love each other and how she always hoped one day, I would change. I thought about my parents and their prayers and how they always believed I would turn around and make something out of my life.

He looked at me with the gun pointed at my head and said, "Do you wanna live, or do you wanna die?"

I looked up at the roof of my vehicle and whispered, "God, help me."

I then looked at that man dead in the eye and said, "I wanna live."

I let these people rob me for all my money, and then with that, they quickly let me go. I drove away angry and upset with myself, thinking about my broken, stained existence and what it even really meant to me. And so I sat in my car and thought about everything I had lost and how much I hated my own being. I was sick and tired of being sick and tired, and I was ready to give in finally and give my life back to God.

A couple of months had gone by, and I was still trying to get my life right with God, but the devil was trying his hardest to destroy me. I still had drugs in my car, and I found them, and I couldn't resist doing them. It was really stupid and pointless, and it already had completely destroyed me. I was so tired of doing it. I sat in my car all night and into the next morning when I finally cried out to God and asked him for his forgiveness. I told him I was tired of living like this, and that I didn't want to live anymore. I had been looking on craigslist for a firearm to kill myself the evening before, but I knew that it was extremely stupid, and it was not gonna happen. I didn't want to spend an eternity in hell where I would suffer forever and ever, and that thought scared me.

I asked God to take this addiction from me; he was my only and last hope. I was tired of running, and I was tired of hurting the people around me. I was a shell of man now, and I never had peace or a good life except for when God was in it. I sat there in that parking lot, staring at this empty abandoned building, crying out to God, when I suddenly felt the warmth of the Holy Spirit surround me, and I felt his goodness, and I finally felt peace.

Staring at this abandoned building, strung out, broken, and empty inside, God finally spoke to me.

He opened up my mind and said, "*That's gonna be your church one day. Go and get ready.*"

I was dumbfounded. I sat there in my car that morning, and I couldn't stop crying and weeping and amazed at what just happened. God had revealed to me at that very moment what I was supposed to be…a preacher…a pastor…a fisher of men. But because of my stubbornness and my waywardness, he let me take a left when I should have stayed right. And this calling on my life had been there since I was kid, and I ignored it the whole time and downplayed it. I had been through so much and hurt so many people, and I felt so much remorse. But God had never forgotten me, and at that moment, he forgave me and gave me a new hope. I was so excited and saddened. At the same time, it was surreal, but I knew that there was no turning back. The enemy wanted my soul, but in the nick of time, God had reached out and saved me from eternal hell fire, and I was not gonna let him down. He had revealed everything to me in one repentful moment that I knew his call was real. His mercy and grace was placed on my broken life. It was so incredible, and I knew he had redeemed me. I was ready for the next step, and I was so excited that I raced home and told my mother. She was happy for me, and I just read the Bible and prayed that day and thanked him over and over. I read the book of John, and I came across the most amazing verse that I believed summed up the whole Bible in a nutshell. "That God so loved the world that he gave his one and only son to die for us. That whoever believes in him would not perish but have everlasting life." John 3:16 was so cliché, but it left me dumbfounded, and I cried, and I cried that day. I was at his mercy, and I knew that I needed to tell my church leaders, and my life was about to change indefinitely.

CHAPTER 9

The Call of God

I couldn't believe what had happened to me and my encounter with the living God and just how merciful he was. I had run from him for twenty-five years, and I was now completely broken, lost, and consumed with sin. But God had saved me in an instant and revealed his plan for my life like the caring father that he was. I owed him everything, and he owed me nothing because he had already given his life for me sum two thousand years prior. And I was told his story at such a young age and had accepted him in my heart and then foolishly walked away. But he had a plan for me, and he was not gonna let me go that easy. My life without him was hard, and I could not go on any further without repenting and asking for his mercy. Every turn was a dead end, and I was lost in sin so much so that without him, I would never be found. I needed to tell my pastor what had occurred, and I was excited because I now knew my path in this life. I was like a lost sheep with nowhere to go and nowhere to hide, but he found me and brought me back into the fold.

The next Sunday, I couldn't wait to tell Pastor Rigo what had happened to me a week prior, and it was an exciting time. I had struggled with giving my life back to God, and it was hard to break free from satan's grip. But I was free and with a new purpose now, and it all finally made sense to me as to why I had run for so long.

As soon as I told my pastor what God had shown me, he embraced me, and he asked, "Are you ready to change your life brother?"

And I was, and so he contacted the other church leaders to council me and help me enroll into Bible college. I was starting from rock bottom, and the only way from here on out was up. But I was glad to have a pastor who never gave up on me and was there for me when I needed him most. He had prayed with me plenty of times before, and he knew of my past. But I was forgiven, and God had set me free from a wicked life of sin, and I was so grateful. The devil had tried hard to destroy my life, and I had let him, but it was God's ultimate plan to bring me back home and ultimately save me.

My ex-wife was going to church again, and we had finally made peace with each other, but she was still struggling to forgive me. It had been a long journey, and she was very skeptical, but we remained friends for our children's sake. I slowly started to rebuild my broken life and put the pieces back together, and it was really tough. Every day I prayed and asked God to make me into what he wanted me to be. I felt whole, and I felt hope again, and that was something that I hadn't felt in so long. Where was God gonna take me? The thought of doing something good for humanity and mankind in general really excited me. It was part of me and had been all my life, but I had run from it. God had designed me in the way he had for a certain purpose, and because I wasn't fulfilling that specific purpose, satan tried to destroy it.

Growing up, I always hated violence, and I always wanted to see good win and evil destroyed. And to watch my life spiral out of control like it did just killed me inside. I knew this wasn't me, and I wasn't supposed to be like this…this broken man that I had become should have not existed. But he did, and now I had the chance to use my life for a greater purpose and give God all the glory. I loved my kids so much, and I had been a terrible father to them…how could I have let them down like this? I had a lot of fixing to do, and it was gonna start with them and felt I owed them a lot. I also felt I had ruined their lives, and I definitely had ruined their childhood, or so it seemed. But luckily, they had a strong faith and beautiful mothers that defended them and took care of them even when I wasn't. I lucked out twice with two great moms who helped me raise my children, and both mothers gave them their very best. And I felt like I owed them a lot too, and I was gonna do my best to show them I was a changed man and a good father. And my praying parents, my mother and father, never gave up on me or stopped praying for me. I believe parents don't hate their children for taking the wrong road; they just pray they turn around before it's too late. I owed them something; and what I owed them was a son who was of sound mind and body. A lost son who was now found, a son who repented and gave his life back to the Lord, and that was the answer to their long worrisome prayers. And I owed myself peace and a relationship with my heavenly Father that I had neglected for so long. I was home, and it felt like I never had left, and it was awesome to be welcomed back with open arms.

So many times before, I would feel very lost and alone, even having my wife and my children all around me. All these years that went by, I couldn't even fathom how I functioned without Christ. I knew the truth, and I walked away from it like it meant nothing to me. But I could never forget or run away from it no matter how hard I tried. And believe me, I tried but to no avail, and I found myself just a shell of a person who no longer loved God, and with that, I no longer loved myself.

It was a long road to recovery…a long winding, bumpy road that I happily took and was ready to travel. I enrolled into Bible college that spring and started to take classes and really started immersing myself in the Word of God. I worked at my church and did every-thing they asked of me and then some. I could feel myself change from the inside out, and I started to become a whole and complete person again. God opened my eyes to this lost world that I lived in, and I came to realize just how much this world needed him. And I was gonna do everything in my power to help recover the lost…the lost like I was once lost.

I had to rebuild and recoup, and that seemed to be a very diffi-cult task at that moment because I had lost so much. I realized that all I had was God, and that was all I ever needed and would ever need in my life. And my children needed their dad, and I needed them, and even though I had their love, I was gonna have to earn their trust back. Piece by piece, I put my life back together, and God had shown his mercy on my life, and I was so grateful. All these years, I had done drugs and the wrong thing, but God had protected me and this calling he had placed on me.

On multiple occasions, I had been stopped by the police when I was under the influence of narcotics, and I had some really close calls. I had always gotten in trouble for all the wrongs I had ever committed, but I never had gotten in trouble for drugs. One of the very last times I had relapsed, I was stopped by police and busted cold turkey with drugs on my lap and in my hand, and my heart was racing. These officers talked to me for what seemed like hours and were oblivious to what I was actually doing. It was right there in front of their face, and both of them didn't see anything. I knew God's mercy had blinded them, but I didn't know how or why he had always protected me from getting a drug charge. Then one day, as I was filling out my paperwork for Bible college, my heart just sank, and I cried out telling God thank you and how amazing he really was. In a small box for my government grant, in black-and-white right in front of my face, I read it.

It said, "If you have ever been charged or convicted of a drug offense, you are not eligible for a government loan or grant."

I was dumbfounded, and I thought back to all those years that I came so close and was never charged or the cops were blinded to it. I was immediately filled with fear because now I knew just how powerful and merciful God really was and what his calling in my life really meant.

I read every book I could find on God, and with every book I read my mind became so much more in tune with Christ and his plan for humanity. I just wanted to tell everybody just how good and merciful he really was. All the suffering in this world could be resolved if we just gave our lives back to him. I learned how the family was under attack by the enemy because broken families directly relate to the degradation of society. And with the degradation of society, the enemy was hard at work preparing the world for the antichrist. And every book I studied and read in the Bible just solidified everything I already knew in my heart. God had designed us to worship him, and he had installed a homing beacon in our bodies. When we are led astray and deceived by the lies of the enemy, that beacon beckons us to come back. That beacon that was going off inside me all the years that I ran from him had become so loud and alarming that I couldn't ignore it any longer. God wants us back, and he will do anything in his power to bring us home and show us his ultimate mercy and grace. I tested all of it, and I will testify to it, and I am forever grateful to Christ, and I will do anything for him. I watched my life transform in front of my eyes, and my children witnessed it too. I just prayed every day for forgiveness and success. I wanted my kids to see me succeed in this life. I felt like a failure, and I hated what I had become, and I knew I never wanted to go back to that life again. So I had to apologize to a lot of people who I disrespected or hurt. I had to swallow my pride and apologize for my horrible behavior when I was so lost in sin. A lot of people didn't want anything to do with me any longer, and that was hard to accept. But I made my peace with it and moved on and stayed in prayer, and God showed me the bigger picture. He had my full attention now, and he started to reveal so much to me that I couldn't believe just how much he loved us. But my relationship with my children was the most important relationship that I needed to fix, and so that's what I decided to do.

My oldest daughter Jocelyn forgave me, and I just told her how much I loved her, and that she meant the world to me. She was twenty-one years old and had been hurt by me plenty because she had seen so much drama and pain caused by me throughout her young years. She was very special to me, and she was always the light to my otherwise dark world. And now I wanted to be a light to her world, and it was gonna take a lot for her to trust me again. She had moved out years prior and moved in with her boyfriend, and she was very independent. She had given her life to God when she was little because my mother had led her to Christ, but Jocelyn had turned away as a teenager. She was very similar to me in a lot of ways, and she also had a lot of her mom in her too, which by the way made her very tough. But she was very supportive of me and had watched me struggle for so long, and she was tired of seeing it. I knew she had a calling in her life also, and God was gonna bring her back. She was my firstborn and was very outgoing, beautiful, and had a lot of friends.

My oldest son Noah and I had our ups and downs, but he forgave me and was a very outgoing positive kid. He was nineteen, very good looking, was into working out, talking to girls, and had a lot of friends. I loved him so much, and I had a lot of regret with how I raised him or better yet didn't raise him, and I felt I wasn't there for him when he needed me the most. I knew I could have been a better father, and I had a lot of remorse that I had to give to God. I remember him being a little boy, and he was always wanting my love and affection, and I was always too busy. I didn't know how to be a father to him when he was younger, but our relationship grew stronger as he got older. I always bought him cool stuff for his birthdays, and he loved going to the movies and watching superhero films with myself and his siblings. He would come work with me in his teens and make extra money, and we became closer. I owed him a lot, and I just wanted him to be proud of me because I was very proud of him and what he was becoming. His dream was to be a US Marine, and he was very proud and determined to make that happen. And I wanted him to make it there, and I always told him to be careful and not get into any trouble like I had. He graduated high school and was working for a summer and had been in contact with a marine recruiter. He was a good kid with a really good personality, and he had a forgiving heart. We made our amends.

And my youngest son Jonah was a straight-A student who loved doing his homework and going to school. He was the kid who looked the most like me but totally took after his mom's side of the family. He was a very caring person and a really good son. He always gave me the benefit of the doubt, and he loved both of his parents equally. I wanted to be a good father to him, and I still had a chance. He had just turned fifteen at the time. This kid was in all the smart classes and had a plan to go to college, and I was very proud of him. He was into wrestling and school sports, and he was not afraid to try anything once, and he never gave up. He was always very close with me as a kid, and I used to buy him video games and superhero toys. We would go see all the superhero movies, and we had a very close relationship. He forgave me for messing up, and he just wanted me to be a good father to him and to his brother and sisters.

Helena was my youngest and probably the most affected by the divorce and my drug addiction that she had to witness. She and I were really close, but after the divorce, she saw her father have a couple mental breakdowns because of the drug use. She was very sensitive and emotional, and she had just turned fourteen at this time. She loved me very much, and I was really sorry that I had hurt her and abused her trust. She just wanted me to straighten up my life and be a good father, and I was determined to do that. She and Jonah went to church with me, and they both had a personal relationship with Christ themselves. I was very proud of her and how beautiful and mature she was, and she had such a good heart. She could be a handful at times with her mother and I, but we loved her very much, and both of us just wanted to see her happy. She loved her friends at school and just really wanted to be accepted and fit in. She was very much into sports and loved playing softball for her school. She was very smart for her age and was an overthinker, so lying to her was not a good thing. Things that didn't add up really bothered her, and she would catch me not telling the truth, and that would upset her. So I just wanted to be truthful with her and honest and be able to look her in the eyes and tell her I was never gonna hurt her again.

It was hard reconciling with my loved ones who I hurt for so many years, and I knew I couldn't turn back to my old ways. My ex-wife was in and out of my life, but she never ran to another relationship like I had. She was going back to school and focusing on her future, and I respected her for that, and she had my full support. She had given her life to God and was going through her own journey and healing from the years of abuse from me and my addiction. I really loved that woman, and I was sorry to have lost her, but we still remained friends, and I was happy with that. The journey ahead of me was going to be long and cumbersome, but I was so ready to take it. The prodigal son had returned and was ready to take on God's highest calling and help recover the lost like I was once lost. I had finally answered the call of God, and he forgave me for all my sins and my dark past. I was no longer lost in sin.

CHAPTER 10

A New Hope

As I sat here reading the Word of God and writing this book, I just had to thank the Lord for his mercy and giving me a new hope. I am in my second year of Bible school, and I am still going very strong, and I am very ambitious with my new found purpose. At the start of the COVID pandemic, God had spoken to me, telling me to write my story down. I didn't understand why, and I told him I was not an author, and I felt my story was embarrassing and very cringeworthy. Why would anyone want to read about my personal struggles? It just didn't make sense. I told him there are much more interesting people and exciting stories to be told, but he kept speaking to my heart and mind. And I couldn't stop thinking about it, and it just became a burning desire to write this true account of my life. This empty hole inside me that I once filled with drugs and infidelities was now filled with the Holy Spirit and the sovereignty of Jesus Christ. I was a different person now, and I knew that there was no going back. And then the COVID pandemic hit, and I just felt the hopelessness of this world and how much it needed Jesus Christ. But all of a sudden, I had plenty of time on my hands because we could no longer go anywhere, and I was homebound.

So I started writing and writing and praying and writing, and this was the final product that God wanted me to put out. He is a loving and caring, merciful God, and he just wants his prodigal sons and daughters to repent and come back to him. And he wants the men and women that he called to preach the good news, to accept it, and to spread it to the masses. It is amazing and so mysterious just how he works his masterful plans to fruition. And we are as preachers and Christians just vessels with open hearts and minds that he uses to tell people what he has done for us through us. Through our personal struggles and issues, he can use our faults and shortcomings to help and teach others. I am just so happy to know that through his atonement on that cross that I have a second chance to right my wrongs. The weight of sin is so heavy, and we as sinners carry that weight on our shoulders every single day of our lives. But we don't have to because we are forgiven, and all we need to do is repent and ask him for forgiveness. But we do not sometimes because we're stubborn, or we don't know that we don't have to carry our sin on our backs forever. That sin was paid for on that cross two thousand years ago and were still forgiven today if we just ask for his forgiveness, and we repent. Satan is the master of lies and deceit, and his greatest trick was convincing the world that sin doesn't exist. Or that God is just a fairy tale that some writer made up to scare people into conformity. It is all lies, and this world has taken a darker turn with the sin of abortion and lawlessness.

I sat at my television watching the riots from police brutality with my children and I knew in my heart that this world was never gonna be the same again. We wear a mask in public, and we have to hide our support for our president out of fear of retribution. This hate for our leaders is only paving the way for the antichrist and his one-world government. Satan is on the attack and wants this nation to be burned down to its core. But at the core is God and his plans for this world are in full effect as we reach the time spoken of in the book of Revelations.

My son Noah is twenty-one years old now and is a US Marine, and he just came back to visit us for the holidays. I am so proud of this young man because he loves God and his country and is willing to lay his life down for it. He is a very brave young man, and his mother and I love him very much and so do all his siblings. He has a bright future ahead of him, and he prays to God and is a believer in

Christ, and I am so thankful. My mother and father are very proud of him also, and we were so happy the day he graduated from boot camp. He is very good looking like his mother, and I am very glad to have him as my oldest son. I see so much hope in this young man, and I pray for him and his safety every single day. Everything he had seen happen with me, he was still able to break free from and succeed with his life. Thank God for his praying grandparents who never gave up praying for him even when I wasn't. He is a strong kid, and I love him so much, and I just can't wait to see what the future holds for him.

His sister Jocelyn is twenty-three now, and she is still in love with her boyfriend and doing great in life. I'm proud of that young woman, and I see so much hope when I look at her. She is very independent and such a hard worker, and I pray for her every single day. I know she has a calling in her life too because she once served God at a young age and like me she turned away. But these turbulent times that we have been enduring has brought her back to her Maker, and I know he is working in her heart. Jocelyn and Noah are very close with their mother who is also doing great. She is happily married and has two more beautiful children, and I pray for her and her family every day. Everything she endured in the past, she overcame, and she still managed to put herself through college and become successful in life. She never let her past define her, and she is the reason my kids are so independent and strong today.

My two youngest children are also doing very well as I write my story, and I couldn't be more proud of them. Jonah, my youngest son, is now seventeen and is preparing to go to a really great college and is sending out applications. He is a straight-A student with a 4.0 GPA and studies really hard and loves doing homework and learning. He is such a great kid and loves God and his family, and I know he has a calling in his life too and is gonna be something great. His sister Helena is sixteen, and she is my youngest and the most outspoken. She is doing great in school and has plans to go into the military like her older brother. She loves God and her friends and is very social and outgoing, and I am very proud of her. I believe God has placed a calling in her life, and I am excited to see what she becomes in the near future. The divorce was hard on them, and they struggled with things for a bit, but God protected them and eased their pain. Their mother is also doing great, and she has put herself through school and is graduating with a degree in business, and I couldn't be more happy for her. It's been four years since our divorce, but we are still very close, and God is doing great things in both of our lives. We met eighteen years ago, and she is still as beautiful today as she was back then. We go to church every Sunday with our children, and she is a very good mother to them.

God is good and doing wonderful things in each of our lives, and we are all so grateful for his mercy and grace. I have seen that woman endure so much because of my sins, and she was lost in sin also, but God found both of us and redeemed us together. We couldn't do this without him, and he is the very reason we are still standing strong today. I love my family very much, and I pray for them every single moment of the day. I am thankful for her and all my children, and God has an ultimate plan for us all. Where does God take all of us from here? I have no idea, but I am so full of hope and optimism. God is the true redeemer in all of our lives, and he can change a willing heart and bring people together through him. He is prolife and pro-marriage, and he wants a family together, not apart. It was never his plan for divorce or infidelity and addictions to take hold, but he can forgive and see us through. I'm just so happy right now, and God is so good, and I thank him every single day for his love and his grace.

He gives us as humans a new hope…a new hope that cannot be taken away by no man or being on this earth. We just gotta believe in him and him alone and give our sins and our shortcomings to our heavenly Father. The story I told is sad and very cringeworthy, but it's a story of true redemption at the cross that he gave his life on. I was running from someone who loved me and only wanted the best for me. And he only wants the best for all of us even with our stubborn and sinful hearts he still loves us. And we push him away like he is nothing, but believe me, he is everything, and our only purpose in life is to love one another and to worship him. And so I accept this man in my heart, and I accept the calling that he has placed on me.

The future looks dim, but with him in my life, I have hope…a new hope. Thank you, Lord, for your mercy and your grace and thank you for this life you have given me. I promise to make the best of it and serve you wholeheartedly. Where I was once lost in sin, I am now found in your presence and your glory. Please show me the rest of the way.

I was fortunate enough to be able to share my story on the 700-club television show and was featured on one of their episodes. It was a great experience, and I am thankful that they chose to film my testimony for the world to see. I knew God wanted me to be fully transparent and candid, and I was, for the sake of helping someone else. People need to hear a story like this, of someone in total despair that turned to God and was given a new hope. That was me, and God wanted to use my personal struggles to evangelize and help others. I attend the School of Urban Missions and have learned so much about the Holy Bible and the Son of God. I will be a licensed minister next year with a bachelors in theology, and I can't wait and look forward to that day soon. God has been good to my family and I, and I am forever grateful for his mercy. I will never turn back or go back to my old ways or my old life. He has brought me through so much, and I am so thankful to him.

CHAPTER 11

You Are! You Are!

You know this year life took a turn for the worse, and the coronavirus happened and changed our lives forever. And everything felt so dreary, and we felt helpless. As Christians, we knew it was time to get on our knees and start praying. God was still in full control, but we were moving into turbulent darker times. People were afraid and started panic buying, causing a toilet paper shortage, and things were getting absurdly out of order. And we watched the rioting on television and living near Denver, Colorado, I witnessed it firsthand. The unrest and anger of these young people who were not going to put up with the police brutality any longer. But then I saw these anarchists start looting stores and destroying property. And innocent people were being assaulted and even killed, and I knew things were never going to be the same. But God was still in full control, and we had to stay in prayer and ask God for his will to be done regardless. I watched all these kids in my Bible college who loved the Lord and were so eager to learn about him rise up. This next generation of pastors and evangelists who were called by God just like me were united for one cause. God was raising up his army to go out and spread the gospel, and it was amazing to watch and be a part of it. The earth is, of course, satan's domain, but the church of Christ definitely holds his dominion back. And I was so amazed witnessing God's army firsthand and the next generation that he is preparing to spread his good news. He loves this world so much, and even as we are moving into the times spoken of in Revelations, the battle for good is still being fought. With the uncertainty of this world at hand, we must stay vigilant and keep fighting the good fight. We must pray for our leaders who are facing so much corruption and disrespect; it is so awful to watch. Our president who backs and supports God's chosen land of Israel is being attacked from all sides. We must pray for this man who I believe is doing the right thing and who God is using for his ultimate glory. Man is fallible, but you have to see through that to see what God is truly doing. It's a battle between good and evil and for the soul of this country. I believe Jesus Christ is returning soon, and the path for the antichrist is being paved as we speak.

I was sitting on my computer one evening when I had gotten an email from a producer I had worked with long ago. He sent me some music that he had produced, and the tracks were all amazing. But one in particular really stuck out to me, and he offered me a great deal, and so I bought the song from him. I played it over and over, and the melody was so beautiful, and I was inspired to write a worship song. I had done music before, but it was so worldly, and God allowed me to fail miserably at it. But this was now, and I was saved, and I was inspired to write a song of redemption in one's darkest hour. God put all the words in my heart, and I wrote them all down verbatim. It was amazing to write something so beautiful and powerful to someone I loved and who had been so merciful to me. The track was written and finished in the matter of weeks, and now I had set out to find a singer. I looked everywhere and asked everyone, and they all just kind of blew me off. Some laughed at me and even the worship team at church said no...I had even offered to pay them.

So I was on my own, and I figured, "Well, I'll sing the song and record it. Then I can submit it to a professional singer to listen to and consider." So I booked time in a professional recording studio and recorded my lyrics on the song. It sounded okay, and so I found some female singers online and submitted it to a few of them. One woman in particular messaged me back, and she really liked the song and wanted to sing on it. She was a single mother and a professional singer who was saved just like me, and we clicked. I brought her down to the studio to record the track, and it came out beautifully. But I kept some of my parts on it, and her voice really brought the whole song together. It was an awesome experience, and I felt so whole and complete. I was not the greatest singer, but it came from my heart and soul. And I believe that's what made the song great, and we had an awesome time doing it. We shot a video, and I put the song up on all streaming platforms, and it was awesome. The day the song was fully mixed and complete, I was driving home and listening to it. I was filled with so much emotion, and I smelled the most beautiful scent ever that words can't explain. It smelled like roses or flowers in my car on the drive home as the song played, and it was so unexplained.

I thank God for all his mercy and his goodness and his love for mankind. Even as the world turns against him since the beginning of time, he has always loved us. The world needs to know this, and I will do everything in my power to tell them…even if I lose my life. Eternity is forever, and we are either going to spend it with him (in heaven) or without him in eternal hell fire. Hell is a real place that God designed for satan and his evil angels, and there is no coming back from there. It's forever and ever and ever, and we can't even fathom what forever really means. All I know is I don't want to go there, and I don't want anyone else in this world to go there, so we must repent now. The stories in the Bible are real, and they are true accounts and tales from multiple people who saw or heard the exact same thing. So how could it not be true? It is 100 percent true. I promise with everything I have in my heart. The Bible tells a story of God's love of this world that he created and the great people who inhabited it. They all turned away from him eventually, and God had no choice but to stop protecting them. And the enemy takes them in death and brings them to their forever home…hell. I have a pretty good imagination of how bad hell can be, and I'm sure I can't even imagine the actual reality of it. It's a horrible place that was not meant for us, but because God is true and blameless…if we don't serve him, we must go there. Thank you, Lord, for your love and your mercy on us; that you came to this earth and died for us. So that we could have a chance to spend eternity in heaven with you. You are holy, and you are perfect, and we worship you…you are…you are.

You Are, You Are
Jason Rangel

The angels worship you…the world has turned on you / I give my life to you / oh Lord, you are / I look at the sky / I stare at the stars. wondering where you are / you're deep in my heart / you're all in my mind / Lord, you are / you are / my savior / my redeemer / God, you're everything to me / my protector / please forgive me / I'm living down on my knees. / This world so dark, and the clouds are gray / I'll search for your light until I find my way / you're the warmth in my heart / you dry the tears from my eyes / you take away all my pain / the only hope in my life. / You died on that cross for the world to see / for every single soul / for all humanity / I give you my heart / my everything / Lord, you are / you are the king of all kings. / I give my life to you / Lord, I worship you / it's all for you Lord / I praise you, Lord / I surrender my life to you / I give you my all / I gave you my all / you gave your life for me / Lord, you died for me / you gave your everything / you gave me everything! / Amen

CHAPTER 12

The Last Days

We are living in turbulent times, and we need God more than ever right now. As this world becomes darker, God's love becomes brighter. Like a beacon of hope, he is calling us to come back home to worship and serve him. Our heavenly Father loves us more than you could possibly imagine. He loves us so much so that he came to this earth in human form for the sole purpose of being a sacrifice. He was the atonement for all of our sins and our worldly desires so that we could be forgiven. And yet this world has rejected him and hates his very name, but we as believers know the truth. We know how merciful he is, and that he just wants us to ask him into our broken, shattered lives. He changes us from the inside out, and he fills that empty hole that's inside all of us with love and hope. And he gives us a peace that we cannot find anywhere else in this whole entire world. A peace that transcends all aggressions and hatred, a peace that will change your life indefinitely. I can attest to all of this, and I will tell everyone about what I know and have learned from my personal mistakes.

This world is satan's, and he is out to kill and destroy because he hates us humans because we are God's creation. We look like God, we are made in his image, and the enemy wants to kill each one of us and take us all to hell as a trophy. But he will not win in the very end, and we are living in the very last days written of in the Holy Bible.

Jesus is coming back real soon, and you can feel this world changing every single day for the worse. It's becoming darker because satan knows his time is short, and he knows the Lord is coming soon.

This nation was built on God, and the Lord blessed it like no other nation ever before. All the other countries were not as prosperous, and the only difference between them and us was our belief in Christ. But as we turn away from God and his holy Word, we are becoming indifferent and intolerable to each other. The enemy's evil plan is to destroy this country from the inside out. Our nation is divided, and a divided nation cannot stand on its own as our enemies sit and wait to devour us. It is ridiculous to put the blame on one individual like the media and leftist would want us to believe. God is and will judge us on our nation's self-servitude and abortion, the millions of unborn babies who are now deceased. Blood is on our hands, and we must repent and turn away from our sins.

Lawlessness and the hate for authority is only setting us up the coming of the antichrist. But all this has to happen so that Jesus Christ can come with his millions of angels beside him to finally take us home. This is not a fairytale, this is a real and true account of what's to come…his return.

I thank everyone who is reading this book, and I thank God for allowing me the opportunity to share my story. Please take every precaution that you possibly can to never go down this same winding road because you don't have too. This is a cautionary tale that God has put on my heart to write down. Everything in this book is true to the best of my knowledge, and I thank God every single day for my life. I pray for anyone that is reading this book that you will find God wherever you are at, and that you repent and accept him in your heart. I pray that you find peace and you experience God's true love and mercy just like I have. I pray for your salvation, and I pray that you make it the end…the ultimate finish line…the gates of heaven. Amen.

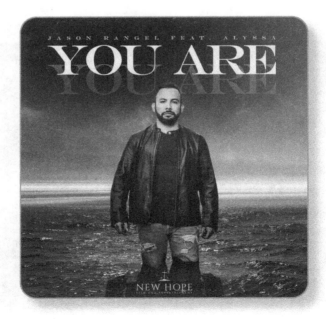

ABOUT THE AUTHOR

Jason Rangel is in his second year at SUM (School of Urban Missions), and he is studying to obtain his bachelor's degree in theology. He has been called to the ministry and will be an official pastor in 2021. He has appeared on *The 700 Club* and has shared his testimony with millions. God continues to do great and amazing things in his life, and he is forever in his debt. He is an author, actor, singer, and the CEO of New Hope Film and Entertainment. He is currently writing a feature film that will win souls and advance the kingdom of heaven.

Any correspondence, please free to email Newhopefilmz@gmail.com.

CPSIA information can be obtained
at www.ICGtesting.com
Printed in the USA
LVHW100239130522
718633LV00005B/123